GUERRILLA MULTILEVEL MARKETING

100 Tactics for Growing Your Network and Advancing to the Top of Your Pay Plan

by
Jay Conrad Levinson,
James Dillehay,
Marcella Vonn Harting

www.GMMLM.com

GUERRILLA MULTILEVEL MARKETING

© 2008, 2007 by Warm Snow Publishers LLC
First Edition

ISBN: 978-0-9710684-9-0
$16.95

Published by:
Warm Snow Publishers
50 Sufi Road, Box 75
Torreon, NM 87061
www.GMMLM.com

Edited by Barbara Brabec
Cover design by James Dillehay

BONUS

Your purchase of this book entitles you to the 21-Day Guerrilla Action Plan. (If you bought from www.gmmlm.com, you will automatically receive each day's actions by e-mail—action steps to help you make the most of the guerrilla system. To start receiving your plan if you bought the book elsewhere, go to www.gmmlm.com/21days/

ACKNOWLEDGMENTS

Thanks to Marcella Vonn Harting, the authors emphasize the use of intentional language. For example, rather than the word "want," which implies lack, we've often inserted the word "choice." We can talk about what you "want" or don't have in your life, or we can remind you to make conscious "choices."

Every day is a new opportunity to move toward the life you envision by reminding yourself in your thoughts, language, and actions that your fate is what you choose, not what your circumstances have—up until now—conditioned you to believe it to be.

If you hold the belief that life is holding you back... that you can't change the way things are, just read the stories in this book. All of our contributors endured hardships and struggles before reaching success in network marketing. They weren't *born* at the top the pay plan.

The authors are grateful to: Margie Aliprandi, Janine Avila, Charlotte Bacon, Barbara Brabec, Richard Brooke, Beatty Carmichael, Fiona Coshman, Doug Firebaugh, Stephanie Forest, Randy Gage, Kosta Gara, Bill Hyman, Dani Johnson, Janet Larson, John David Mann, Keith McEachern, Lorna Rasmussen, Sherry Roden, Bonnie Ross-Parker, Dr. Joe Rubino, Tim Sales, and Mary Billeter Young for their motivating stories.

Special thanks go to Kosta Gara for his stirring foreword, Nicki Keohohou of DSWA for her introductions to many of our contributors, and Barbara Brabec for her keen editing.

TABLE OF CONTENTS

STORIES

FOREWORD

I still remember that cold, November evening that changed my life. Just imagine-someone had generously taken time out of his busy schedule just to teach me how I could succeed in Multilevel Marketing. I was excited about the knowledge I had just acquired. I needed to put that knowledge into action NOW.

Yet despite all that I learned that night, I knew there was still so much more to know. I had passion! I was bursting with enthusiasm! But I was also ignorance on fire. I desperately needed to acquire greater knowledge if I was to be successful in this new venture.

I went to bed that evening, dizzy from all the plans running through my head. I could barely keep up with my next thought. Sleep! How could I sleep that night when I was on the threshold of my new life?

One thing I did not need the next morning was an alarm clock. I raced out of bed, barely gulping down a coffee and quick breakfast, and rushed to the nearest bookstore. Anxiously, I waited outside the door for the store to finally open.

Rushing to the business section, I searched in vain for that one MLM manual that would provide me with all the information I needed to know to get started. Finding books on MLM was not a problem. But all of these books were too specialized on a single topic. My mind continued to race—how many of these books would I need to buy? How much will they cost? Where will I find the time to read them all?

WHY CAN'T I FIND ONE BOOK THAT COVERS EVERYTHING I NEED TO KNOW TO GET STARTED?

This is the one dilemma that has dogged all new entrants to MLM. That is, until now.

Guerilla Multilevel Marketing is just THE operations manual you need to get started. In this one book, you'll find over 100 tactics offered by some of the most renowned leaders in the industry who have over three centuries of accumulated knowledge to share. It is like having the best in the industry there to mentor you whenever you need them.

Even seasoned networkers will find this book a valuable resource. With all its wisdom gathered in an indexed format, you can quickly find solutions to many problems instantly at your fingertips. Nothing is better than learning from those who have conquered many of the same issues you may be facing now!

I congratulate *Guerilla Multilevel Marketing* for harnessing the knowledge of so many industry leaders to put together the first all-inclusive MLM business-training manual. And I applaud the industry leaders who volunteered their time to help others succeed. I am proud to be associated with each of you!

Kosta Gara
www.kostagara.com

CHAPTER 1

Why Guerrilla Multilevel Marketing

---

*"It is impossible to win the race unless
you venture to run, impossible to win the
victory unless you dare to battle."*
~ Rich DeVos, co-founder Amway ~

Your network marketing business is crying out for help. You've exhausted your warm list. Prospects won't come to your opportunity meetings. Conference calls aren't inspiring your team to act. Ads are costing you money, but not paying for themselves. You would quit except there's nothing much to give up.

Despite the lack of life signs in your business, you feel network marketing still holds a promise. It's just that some missing piece of the network marketing puzzle continually eludes you; prevents you from entering network marketing heaven.

That missing piece is the problem. It can be neatly summed up in the words: *you don't know what you don't know.*

What would it be like if you could discover what it is you don't know that successful network marketers do and put that knowledge to work for you today?

No Experience Required

Here's something almost everyone in the network marketing industry does know: the majority of newly enrolling distributors don't have a business background or a clear understanding of marketing. Nevertheless, recruits are still being urged to treat network marketing as a business.

Is it any wonder that new signups have a fear in the back of their mind, because they really don't know what a business is or how to run one? How long will they linger before the fear tells them to *run?* Hint: 90 percent of new distributors quit their first year.

How many more distributors would stay with network marketing if they were confident in the beginning that they didn't have to know how to run a business to succeed at network marketing? What if you could present them with a system that was easy for anyone, even someone without business experience, to learn and teach?

Leaving Money on the Table

An obstacle for many distributors is the MLM culture of conformity—an expectation that everyone must follow the herd or be abandoned. A *one-way-for-everybody* attitude leaves a lot of money on the table.

The reality is that most people in network marketing do the business a little differently from each other anyway. Evidence shows that you will earn more money by teaching a system that supports variety and is suitable to different personality types. *Guerrilla Multilevel Marketing* offers a way to support and enable distributors to thrive using tactics they can apply their personal strengths to.

In his bestselling book, *The Wave 4 Way to Building Your Downline*, author Richard Poe cites a 50 percent boost in sales and 15 to 20 percent increase in retention of people when offering downline members multiple ways of prospecting.

Guerrilla Multilevel Marketing provides you with a menu of 100 marketing tactics, many of which are free and low cost. It reveals the mysterious missing piece of the network marketing puzzle. It provides a system to make marketing a clearly understood, step-by-step process.

Guerrillas map out the coming months and years which eliminates anxiety about what's ahead. How much more could you achieve if you can replace fear of the unknown with certainty about your network marketing future?

Marketing is Every Communication

The fastest way to clear up any confusion about what network marketing is as a business is for you to recognize that **marketing is every communication you make** about your product or opportunity.

As you begin to apply the guerrilla approach, you may be surprised to discover just how many communications you make every day which are, in fact, marketing opportunities.

Marketing is all about communicating and it's all about *every* communication, including the way you answer your phone, the color and type of shoes you wear, and your readiness to smile and greet a stranger you just met.

Marketing includes the design of your business card and the fact that you even have a business card on hand to give someone at a moment's notice. Marketing also includes how quickly you answer e-mails and return phone calls. It's also about communicating consistently and frequently.

Using the guerrilla tactics in this book, you'll discover how to breathe marketing power into all your communications. You'll learn how to utilize the power of always-on marketing.

Growing Your Warm List

Your upline wisely begins your entry into networking by encouraging you to make a warm list of everyone you know. They know from experience that by getting you started contacting people who know you, your first efforts at network marketing will be aimed at the people who like and trust you.

Regardless of how many people you know, your initial warm list runs out. From then on, growth depends on consistently finding and bringing more people into your network. Your business requires an incoming flow of people—people with whom to communicate and to grow relationships.

Guerrilla Multilevel Marketing tactics will generate streams of prospects. As a guerrilla, you'll learn ways to transform those prospects into new friends and then into life-long customers and some into successful business builders.

Ways Guerrilla Marketing Differs

Following are twelve ways in which guerrilla marketing differs from conventional marketing:

1. Instead of investing money in the marketing of your product or opportunity, you are investing your **time, energy, and imagination.** This makes *Guerrilla Multilevel Marketing* perfect for network marketers with small budgets and big dreams.

2. Instead of using guesswork in network marketing, you are using the science of **psychology**—actual laws of human behavior.

3. Instead of concentrating on leads, responses, or sales volume, **the size of your compensation check** is the yardstick by which you measure your marketing's effectiveness.

4. Instead of being oriented to large businesses with big bank accounts for advertising, guerrilla marketing is geared to **individuals** with limited resources.

5. Instead of counting sales, guerrilla networkers count the number of new **relationships**, because they know that people buy from people they like.

6. Instead of believing that single marketing tactics such as buying leads, renting lists, or mailing

CDs are enough, guerrilla networkers know that **marketing combinations** get customers to buy and distributors to act.

7. Instead of encouraging you in only a few ways of prospecting, guerrilla marketing provides you with **100 different marketing weapons**, allowing you to build the business in a way that suits your personality.

8. Instead of being unintentional by using mass marketing methods, guerrilla marketing is **always intentional**, embracing all the details, even how you answer your phone.

9. Instead of growing linearly by adding new customers one by one, guerrilla network marketers **grow geometrically** by using the powerful leveraging tactics explained in the guerrilla marketing system.

10. Instead of thinking about how much money you can make off of others, guerrilla marketing is thinking of **what you can give** in the way of free support to help customers, team members, and prospects.

11. Instead of disregarding technology, guerrilla marketing encourages you to be **techno-friendly,** because ignoring technology will lead to extinction these days.

12. Instead of being "me marketing" and talking about your issues and goals, guerrilla multilevel marketing is **"you marketing"** and talks about your prospect's needs.

Think Leverage

Network marketing lets you leverage your time and efforts by getting paid on the time and efforts of others. Guerrilla marketing magnifies the power of leveraging by teaching how to automate your lead gathering, reach hundreds more prospects, and even how to get prospects to pay you for your marketing.

Guerrilla marketing will work as a powerful leveraging tool for you when:

1. You are using your company's products and are

completely sold on their benefits.

2. You are committed to network marketing as a business lifestyle.

3. You are willing and eager to learn.

4. You won't give up until you're dead.

Think Fun

Everyone desires fun, whether they acknowledge it or not. Play is *worked* out of us as we pass through school into the job market, but the desire for play never leaves. It just gets buried by fear that we won't be taken care of.

It's often difficult for new distributors to believe they can actually play for a living, but thousands of veteran network marketers are living the proof every day. Guerrillas enjoy their business activities, because they follow the system outlined in this book which takes away the confusion and uncertainty of what to do to grow.

Getting the Most from This Book

The power of *Guerrilla Multilevel Marketing* reveals itself by creating a circle which gathers prospects, who become leads, and then loyal customers and distributors returning to you again and again. Start your guerrilla entrepreneurial training:

- Go through the book reading the twenty-four stories from high-earning network marketing leaders for inspiration
- Read the book through again thoroughly from beginning to end
- Get your 21-Day Guerrilla Action plan. Each day you'll get an action step to help you make the most of this book. Go to www.gmmlm.com/21days/
- Create your own 7-sentence guerrilla marketing plan as outlined in Chapter 3
- Review each chapter's tactics (at the end of each

chapter) and filling in the checklist so you can go back and add appropriate tactics to your marketing plan (download the complete 100 tactic checklist at www.gmmlm.com/tactics.htm)

• Schedule your guerrilla marketing calendar
• Take actions based on your calendar
• Measure and evaluate your results
• Make choices about your future marketing based on results, not on guesswork.

Guerrilla Multilevel Marketing helps you replace confusion with clarity. Guerrilla marketing is results-based. It puts you in control of how you grow your business, starting with learning how to work *on* your business, not just *in* it.

CHAPTER 2

UNDERSTANDING STRATEGY AND TACTICS

"A sly rabbit will have three openings to its den."
~ Chinese Proverb ~

Before presenting you with a list of guerrilla multilevel marketing how-tos to build your business, understand that all of the tactics you eventually decide to use will have a greater impact when they are marched forward from strategy.

Knowing where you are going and being excited about that vision will empower each action step you take. It will also help make the journey an enjoyable one, rather than a series of obligations or chores.

In his book, *The E-Myth Revisited*, Michael Gerber reports that most business owners tend to work *in* their business, not *on* it. Entrepreneurs start off with big dreams, but quickly become employees in their own enterprise. They have not learned to see that the business itself is a product.

You may already be working as hard as you can and getting nowhere. Yet there are millionaires and billionaires who put in as much time as you do at work while getting paid much more than you. So what's the difference?

Working smarter pays better than working harder. Creating strategies is working *on* your business. Investing part of your time working *on* your business instead of always working *in* your business gets you out of the trenches and into the high ground, where you can see what's going on.

Some people are very confident and comfortable being in the moment with others without having a predefined aim. If you are one of those people, you don't necessarily go into meetings with an objective—you have inner trust that you will feel your way through and a relationship will evolve.

Schedule in a couple of hours every week where you strategize your growth. Working *on* your business means putting time into training so you'll be better at all the aspects of network marketing, including product knowledge, rapport building, getting people to commit, and qualifying leads.

Strategy means creating a vision of what your aim is so that your tactical actions interweave and support the bigger picture.

You've probably heard and read how important it is to have written goals for your business. Super-charge the goal-setting process by creating objectives for all the areas of your business, like prospect interactions, distributor training, personal growth and every other area of network marketing.

"The general who wins the battle makes many calculations in his temple before the battle is fought. The general who loses makes but few calculations beforehand."

~ Sun Tzu ~

Imagine strategy as building a business model you could franchise and sell to others. This is essentially what duplicable network marketing is about—developing a model system for running a turnkey business you can teach others to profit from.

Here's a list of suggested key areas of your network marketing business to invest at least one hour per week strategizing on:
- Your own personal growth and ongoing training
- How you interact with prospects
- How you interact with customers
- How you interact with distributors
- How you follow up
- How you train others
- Your customer service procedures
- Your arsenal of promotional tools
- Your market and product knowledge

Even without strategy, you can see results just by applying tactics randomly. However, you can get exponentially better results by creating strategies which relate to and energize the steps you take to grow.

You can imitate the actions of MLM high-earners, but you'll get bigger checks faster by learning how they think, how they strategize.

A strategy clarifies your aim; tactics tell you how to get there. You can have more than one strategy for achieving your goals and multiple tactics for getting there.

For instance, let's say you choose to achieve better results from your interactions with others. Eleven potential strategic goals you might seek from your communications are:

Guerrilla Affirmation

I make all my communications with prospects, customers, and team members part of my marketing. My words, feelings, and activities are **intentional** and propel me toward my goals.

1. To be the most sought out expert in your market for information
2. To make every product buyer and distributor feel like you are taking care of them as a client instead of just making a sale
3. To increase the size of each transaction
4. To instill a sense of urgency that speeds up the buying process
5. To upsell other products or services the customer had not yet considered
6. To get customers on an autoship program
7. To generate referrals
8. To create trust in your company's brand
9. To inspire customer and distributor loyalty
10. To create relationship-bonding with customers and distributors
11. To acquire contact information

How you think about your business may evolve over time and experience. Your aims and goals will change as your income and opportunities grow.

A successful strategy can be as simple as getting to know people better. Marcella didn't start out planning to build a large organization. Her success led her to realize that the real product in network marketing is people.

Marcella's Story

When my little girl was born, she swallowed meconium, the tar-like bowel movement of infants; it poisoned her system. At seven months, she contracted a severe case of pneumonia and literally died in my husband's arms as we rushed to the hospital. God miraculously gave her back to us. We lived in the critical care unit of the hospital for ten days.

When she was three, a team of doctors told me she was retarded and nothing could be done for her. I refused to accept their diagnosis. I started investigating alternative health and nutrition. If someone said they had something to help my daughter, I was right there checking it out. One day I got a phone call from a friend, Mary Young, co-founder of Young Living, asking me if I knew anything about aromatherapy.

I found research by a Dr. Lapraz examining the effects of essential oils. I was so impressed I started experimenting with various essential oils with my daughter. My husband and I were overjoyed as we saw significant positive changes in her abilities.

The changes were so substantial, her teachers and the parents of her friends started asking me what I was doing. It was amazing to watch my daughter's progress. She went from being diagnosed as retarded to graduating from college with a degree.

During those years I was so focused on helping people feel better, I wasn't interested in making money. It wasn't until my check started getting big that I even realized I had a business. I had been plugging away through all sorts of company changes, hanging in there like a bulldog, until one day I looked at my six-figure commission check and I realized I had a successful business.

I felt such a strong gratitude and moral responsibility to support the people in my organization, I sat down and cried. The reason I did this was not the company, or the products or the money; it was the people! And *the* reason for my success *is* my relationships with people.

My relationships have taken me to the top in my organization as a Crown Diamond, with over $4 million sales volume per month. The level of success relies on dedication and skill level. If you would like to create life-long happiness and success, get to know PEOPLE, including yourself.

Marcella Vonn Harting is co-author of Guerrilla Multilevel Marketing *and* "Yes No Maybe" Chronobiotic Nutrition *and author of* The Harting Training System. *She is a Crown Diamond, trainer and top earner in Young Living Essential Oils. See* www.MarcellaVonnHarting.com

The next chapter helps you create an overall strategy of your marketing in a written plan which can be summed up in seven sentences.

"People take different roads seeking fulfillment and happiness. Just because they're not on your road doesn't mean they've gotten lost."
~ H. Jackson Browne ~

CHAPTER 3

SEVEN SENTENCES TO A PROFITABLE FUTURE

"You read a book from beginning to end. You run a business the opposite way. You start with the end, and then you do everything you must to reach it."
~ Harold Geneen ~

High-earning network marketers take actions based on a marketing plan—a plan that allows them to stay in control of their business. This chapter lets you create your own personalized blueprint for success in seven sentences.

A marketing plan can be brief enough to be written on one or two pages. It should be simple and clear enough that you are able to understand it, use it, and update it as your experiences over time dictate.

Your cost of creating a marketing plan is zero in dollars and a small amount of thinking that will pay you back for years to come.

TACTIC 1. YOUR 7-SENTENCE MARKETING PLAN

The following seven sentences will help you focus your intentions and activities. They will guide your steps in moving from inner vision to outward reality.

Your 7-Sentence Marketing Plan will clarify:

1. The most desired results your marketing will achieve

2. The benefits users of your product or opportunity will receive

3. Who your niche audience is

4. Which tactics you will use to accomplish your aims

5. The niche you choose to be known for

6. What your true identity is

7. How much you will budget for marketing.

How you answer these questions will shape your marketing action steps, so take time to think about your answers.

For each product or service you promote, create a separate plan. If you intend to focus on getting business builders as well as new customers, write a marketing plan for each aim, because reaching your two audiences will require different activities and timing.

Step 1: What is the most desired result of your marketing?

What will your marketing achieve? In other words, when someone comes across your message, what action would you have them take?

Do you choose for people to buy your product? Do you choose for people to call you? Do you choose for people to join as distributors? Do you choose for your team to become more active?

Write the most desired result(s) of your marketing:

_____

_____

_____

_____

Step 2: What benefits will buyers of your product or opportunity experience which set you apart from competing offers?

What's in it for your prospect? What will a customer get by buying your product? What will a distributor gain by signing up with you?

List every benefit you can come up with. To start, you can find many of your product or opportunity's benefits in your company's promotional material.

You can uncover a wealth of benefits from satisfied users. Discover hidden benefits your product delivers only happy consumers will tell you about.

List benefits, not features. For example, your nutritional supplement may be a powerful antioxidant, but that is a feature. The benefit is more vitality and slowing down the effects of aging. Customers aren't buying the antioxidant, they are buying anti-aging.

Benefits can also be expressed as ways to avoid pain. People are more motivated to stop their pain than they are to find positive solutions. Increase your marketing's response rates by describing what the person will lose if he fails to correct his problem.

When looking for benefits to describe your opportunity, think of how network marketing provides supplemental income, opportunities for personal growth, learning management skills, enhanced self-esteem, and increased confidence.

List your benefits. Think of each benefit as a hot button. The more buttons you can press, the more prospects will commit.

_____

_____

_____

_____

_____

_____

_____

_____

The next chapter on niche marketing will help you learn how to identify even more benefits of your product or service that make your marketing stand out from the competition.

Step 3: Who is your audience?

Who is your marketing going to reach? If your answer is *everyone*, guess again. Just because anyone could use your product doesn't mean they are likely to. Be prepared to talk to everyone as if they were your audience, but avoid wasting money and time marketing to questionable prospects.

When you know exactly who is most likely to buy your product, you can confidently plan a marketing campaign you can afford and one which will yield profitable returns.

Your ideal customers are those who seek products that satisfy their particular needs. Define your ideal customer by sex, age, income, hobbies, purchasing habits, and any other demographic fact that helps you direct your message to their interests. The following chapter will give you ideas for identifying your customer. You may discover many distinct audiences to market to. Describe them:

_____

_____

_____

_____

_____

_____

Step 4: What tactics will you use to reach your audience?

This book describes 100 guerrilla multilevel marketing tactics. At the end of each chapter from here on, there is a checklist of tactics that lets you choose those most appropriate for you. Read through all the tactics first, fill in the checklists, and then return here to fill in this part of your plan (download the complete 100 tactic checklist at www.gmmlm.com/tactics.htm.)

After exploring all of the 100 tactics, you may find only fifty or sixty tactics appropriate for your product or opportunity, or that fit your personality. But knowing about all of the 100 tactics assures you haven't ignored a potential way to bring in more business.

Though your list may be long, you won't launch all the tactics at the same time. Working from your marketing calendar (see later in this chapter) you will learn how to schedule your action steps.

When training your team, find out what someone is good at and recommend he or she applies related tactics. Help people shine at what they do well before asking them to grow out of their comfort zone.

Marketing is never static; it's the ongoing, dynamic lifeblood of a business. Hopefully, you will come up with even more ideas for marketing than we mention in this book. Keep adding tactics to your list and deleting those that don't work. Remember: tactics that are inappropriate for you may be perfect for someone else on your team.

List your tactics:

_____

_____

_____

_____

_____

_____

_____

_____

_____

_____

_____

_____

_____

Step 5: What do you choose to be known for? What is your niche?

What is the niche that you would have people remember you for? Does your compensation plan pay out more bonuses than any other company? Is your product the only one that solves a particular problem? Does it solve a person's problem faster, easier, or cheaper than competing products?

What makes your offer memorable:

_____

_____

_____

Step 6: What is your identity?

Image can easily be confused with identity. Businesses use marketing to project a favorable public image. The highly publicized scandals of Enron, Xerox, and Worldcom have changed their images forever.

Consumers are hungry to do business with those who present a true identity, one that reflects values of honesty, integrity, and service.

Though corporations can hide behind huge ad campaigns, network marketers are face to face with prospects and customers daily. People you meet are quick to pick up on false pretenses. They are more willing to do business with you when they trust you are who your marketing messages represent you to be.

Describe your true identity below. What values will you bring into your daily business?

_____

_____

Step 7: Budget how much you will invest in marketing.

What percentage of your compensation check will go back into your marketing? This amount should be expressed as a percentage of your expected income for the next year.

How much should you budget for marketing? It depends on how fast you choose to grow. How many new distributors can you support, train, and follow up with each week? There's no point in bringing in more people than you can realistically work with, because many of those you abandon will drop out as soon as you start ignoring them.

Later in this book, we'll teach you how to track and measure your marketing to know where your dollars pay off before deciding to invest more. If you discover a tactic that proves to consistently produce more income than it costs, you would naturally invest more, as long as the results continue to justify the expense.

Write your marketing budget for the next year:

Marketing to those who have already bought from you is cheaper and faster than trying to get new customers. One study showed that it costs an average of five times as much money to acquire new business as it does to retain existing customers.

To maximize your resources, divide your marketing budget as follows:

1. 60 percent to existing customers
2. 30 percent to qualified prospects
3. 10 percent to the universe of people you've never met

The mission of this book is to provide you ways to expand your list of prospects—moving them from the impersonal universe into your warm list.

Tactic 2. Your Marketing Calendar

After you have chosen the marketing tactics most appropriate to use to reach your goals, create a marketing calendar to organize and schedule how you will carry out your promotional action steps.

Unpredictability is a major cause of stress for many business owners. A marketing calendar protects you from the unknown by providing a blueprint for your future. Your marketing calendar gives you the big picture—showing you how all the elements of your plan work together.

Imagine your business before using a marketing calendar as being like looking out a window that's so clouded you cannot see what's going on. Your calendar clears the window and makes everything apparent.

Your calendar helps you avoid costly shotgun marketing and engage in laser-focused, profitable campaigns you can track and measure. It prevents you from leaving anything out of the picture.

Your marketing calendar renews your commitment and your team's commitment as well since everyone can see their efforts as an investment in a consistent plan.

The most useful calendar will spell out each promotion, activity, and event. Include the marketing cost for each tactic along with the effects that came from the event. By doing this, you will always know which promotions were productive and which ones to change or drop, thus eliminating the guesswork when it comes to marketing dollars.

"How does a project get to be a year behind schedule? One day at a time."
~ Fred Brooks ~

Guerrilla Affirmation

I have a focused, written *marketing plan* which clarifies my unique product benefits and shapes my promotional actions.

On the following page is an example of a marketing calendar. In the example, several activities are planned. Download a marketing calendar template at www.gmmlm.com/calendar.doc. Adjust your calendar to fit the hours and days you will devote to growing your business.

After you have had time to measure the results of your activities, go back and grade them as you would a school report card. Grade "A" is excellent and Grade "F" fails. After grading, you can quickly assess what's working (to do more of) and what's failing to produce (eleminate or improve.)

Google offers a free program you can use to make your events viewable to others. It's a public calendar at www.calendar.google.com. This a free way to keep your team members up to date on what's coming in the way of trainings, conference calls, and company events.

TACTIC 3. YOUR CONSISTENT ACTION

Talk with anyone in your upline who has earned big checks and they'll tell you they *consistently* approached prospecting to reach the upper levels of the pay plan.

Well-conceived marketing isn't a guessing game, it's a blueprint. However, like any blueprint, it's useless

Sample Marketing Calendar

Date:

Tactic	Cost	Action	Result
Warm list	0	Call 20 prospects on warm list to invite to home reception next Tuesday	**GRADE=C** 8 people agreed to come; 6 showed up; 1 person signed up as distributor; 2 people bought product at event
Testimonials	0	Gather product testimonials and create hand out	**GRADE=A** listed 12 testimonials
Inserts	875	Order inserts and call to set up for inserts to go out in Sunday newspaper	**GRADE=D** 5,000 inserts went out; 35 people called back; 23 people requested samples; 6 people ordered; 2 signed up as distributors
Research studies	5	Make copies of research studies and mail to 12 previous customers who haven't ordered recently	**GRADE=B** mailed to 12; 3 people called; 1 person placed new order
Classified ad	600	Write and place biz op ad in USA Today	**GRADE=B** 17 call backs; 5 people requested samples; 1 new sign up
Training call	0	Call team members about Monday eve. training call	**GRADE=A** 8 people agreed to be on call; 7 were on

unless you make a commitment and follow through with taking action regularly.

Guerrilla network marketers build one customer at a time, one distributor at a time. They know that if they have a life-changing product, an exciting compensation plan, and a parent company that practices exemplary customer service, it is inevitable that people they talk to will sign up. If one person will sign up, then a second person will sign up. If two will sign up, then a third will sign up.

Large organizations grow over time. Large organizations develop because the builder takes consistent actions and is committed to a plan. Sometimes they grow in spite of the odds against you, like with Stephanie Forest.

Moving In, Moving Up
by Stephanie Forest

It's kind of crazy in a way to think that I made it to the top rank of our company in just over a year and a half. I hadn't worked in a while, choosing to be with my young son. It made no apparent sense that I could move to the top level in the company because, except for a flamboyant, entrepreneurial and gorgeous hair stylist, my dear front line business builders were also mothers like me with very small children. These exceptionally bright optimistic women had literally no business experience at all, and one beautiful singer from a foreign country was just getting her green card.

The husband of one of the youngest mothers was an angelic hippy-style dude who traveled widely amongst circles of friends and boasted about never having earned more than a three-figure income in any given year. Then there was a really nice woman, a New York City office manager I had met on a Sufi retreat. She lent me four thumbtacks and asked me to return them at the end of the retreat. You see what I mean about making it to the top?

So what in the world happened to motivate our little crew to keep going and earn a substantial residual income and free products?

The first most prevalent issue was the core ingredient in our products quickly and obviously transformed the health of those who consumed it.

Secondly, I sensed at the beginning of my initiation into network marketing that I was going to reach the highest level, and I held an imprint like a deep unshakeable conviction within myself that it was only just a matter of time. The distributors in both my downline and upline inspired me all along the way.

We slipped effortlessly into roles that held a universal unconditional loving and accepting orientation: no one is left out. No matter what their current status in life or struggles with self-esteem, we held an intrinsic belief in our distributor's ability to seriously make their lives far richer and healthier on all levels. This was our bottom-line attitude and basically we never departed from it.

We discovered that we didn't need substantial amounts of money to make money. Our goals were to see others succeed. We trusted the laws of attraction—the great source of all abundance brings to us the prosperity and joy we dream into being. We are top-level execs already. We just have to step into the role. These were the fundamental belief systems we employed and, while essentially idealistic, they kept working for us.

Practically speaking, we also saw that one of the best ways to bring an organization together is to create and send out a personal newsletter. This remains true today. A newsletter assures our customers that their fiercely loyal upline is still buying and using the products as well.

I introduced a series of strategic CEO actions with my first level leaders and their execs who were close to me. It evolved naturally, an obvious extension from mothering skills. It's what I call the "Move-In Method" (M-IM). It includes simple repetitive actions that are the secret behind my success and my ability to move up the ladder of success against formidable odds.

Soon after I signed up, the most pro-active business builder in our company came to my home to present a training seminar. Transmitting a gem of wisdom, this upline leader said, "Keep it simple," and so I did. Serving healthy nutrition became my way to honor this message.

When people came over, I introduced them to our line by making shakes and offering supplements throughout the day. Soon we became friends as together we connected to something profoundly positive. Often, I invited my friends to stay the night and continued to serve them more yummy smoothies and nutritionals until eventually they began to see how good they were in comparison to what we buy at market.

After they got a feel for the product, many times I would be invited to go over to their house. As per the M-IM, if they lived at a distance, I stayed overnight. Of course I brought product. Returning again to feed and nurture, and explaining more about the products while our children played around us, proved to be a simple and easy way to demonstrate how we could make money from home, get healthy, and enjoy ourselves in each other's company. It was total win/win/win.

Stephanie Forest reached Double Diamond in her network marketing company in 18 months. She is also healer, educator, author of a monthly newspaper column, and hosts her own weekly community radio show. See www.askheaven.com.

Checklist for this Chapter's Tactics

Place a check in the appropriate column for determining how or if you will use a tactic. Then return to your 7-sentence marketing plan - see Chapter 3 - and fill in the appropriate tactics in Step 4 of your plan.

Tactics In This Chapter	Using Well	Using, But Needs Work	Not Using	Not Right At This Time
1. Marketing Plan				
2. Marketing Calender				
3. Consistent Action				

CHAPTER 4

NICHE OR MISS

*"Find out where the people are
going and get there first."*
~ Mark Twain ~

Is everyone a candidate for your product or service? Conventional network marketing says yes. Unfortunately, applying this tenent has derailed many distributors. The effect of treating everyone as a target is that everyone will treat you as a salesperson. And what do *you* do when *you* encounter a salesperson?

This chapter teaches you how to make the best use of your resources by communicating your offer to those most likely to be interested by:
• Identifying ideal customers by niche
• Seeking business-minded prospects

TACTIC 4. IDENTIFYING IDEAL CUSTOMERS BY NICHE

Just because anyone and everyone *can* use your product or extra income plan, it doesn't follow that they are all *likely* to do so. Why waste your time attempting to sell to everyone and facing "no" after "no," when you can have droves of customers who are looking for exactly what you offer?

Of course, you should be prepared to respond to every person as if he could be a customer. But before launching into a pitch about your product, learn about your prospect. A chance meeting could lead to someone trying your product for the first time. That person could experience life-changing results and start referring others who get involved as distributors. High-earning network marketers are always prepared to promote spontaneously.

The average person is exposed to several hundred marketing messages every day. People block out or ignore most of these messages because the information doesn't pertain to their immediate problems. However, if an ad or an e-mail or a friend speaks to a person's exact situation, the subconscious starts to pay attention.

Guerrillas earn bigger checks because they target niche customers. A niche can be identified by an activity or community organized around a specific interest. Members tend to feel there's something special about the group, the topic, or their involvement in it. Niche groups are natural networks because members interrelate.

Your Experience and Interests

When brainstorming niches for your products, think about topics you can personally connect with. Look for activities you are excited about or have life experience with. From your involvement with a career, a health challenge, a hobby, or education, you may already know a great deal about a subject. Even a minimal knowledge will expose you to resources from which you can research what you don't know.

Members of a niche audience can be reached through their affiliation with a topic. For instance, doctors interested in alternative medicine subscribe to newsletters and journals on the subject, network with other practitioners in the community, and advertise their services according to their specialties.

Browse online and library directories for learning more about your field. Almost every topic has resources outlined in a directory, from which you could locate, buyers, organizations, publications, and more. For example, if you seek buyers of business opportunity books, look up business book catalogs in the *National Directory of Catalogs,* available in many libraries. These catalogs rent their list of buyers.

If your offer lends itself to a technical audience, look for groups formed around computer and electronic users. Don't mail those techies an offer for skin care—it's a waste of time and money.

Look at how your product solves specific problems. For instance, Jim found that using his product before a weight-lifting workout increased his endurance for repetitions and reduced muscle soreness. Just relaying those particular benefits when speaking with prospects who were fitness buffs doubled his sales.

"Friendship is born at that moment when one person says to another: What! You too? I thought I was the only one."
~ C. S. Lewis ~

Explore your niche audience and you will discover their pains. You will become aware of what issues are important to them—what problems they long to solve.

Defining your niche makes it easier to identify your benefits. For instance, retail business owners suffer from non-paying customers. A benefit to them would be saving time and money using a legal service to go after bad debts.

Your products may benefit more than one audience. Create a distinct marketing campaign for each niche audience. Your sign-up rate will skyrocket, because your message is directed to people looking for the solutions your product offers.

Describing Your Customer

Income, gender, race, age, geographic location, hobbies, marital status, education and number of children are all demographic factors that can help you make decisions on who to market to. The following demographics describe targetable niche audiences.

Gender

Women make more than 83 percent of consumer buying decisions. Women dominate the ranks of network marketing and direct selling. In general, women outrank men in starting businesses. The Center for Women's Business Research reports:

- One in eleven adult women is an entrepreneur.
- The estimated growth rate in the number of women-owned businesses was nearly double that of all firms.
- Female entrepreneurs account for 70 percent of new business startups.
- 86 percent of women entrepreneurs say they use the same products and services at home as they do in their businesses.
- Women use the Internet more than men.
- Women emphasize relationship building as well as gathering facts.

Truth or Dare
by Janet Larson

It seems like a lifetime ago when I was a young or not so young lady – filled with fears, insecurities, fragile in constitution and controlled by others who told me how life needed to be.

Today, my picture looks a whole lot brighter having made the decision to step out of the 'box' and into this grand playing field called LIFE. Here I have run up against few boundaries other than those I have imposed upon myself. I dared myself to dream and then I dared myself to do and what has come of that is a healthy dose of lessons and pleasures as I continue to co-create with my God – a life rich in health, peace, relationships and lifestyle. What's not to love about that, right?! The universe holds the same gifts in store for you if you are willing to let go of what isn't working in your life and grab hold of what will work and then *simply* do what it takes to create the experience of success.

Initially I called upon wiser, more experienced people to show me the way. But not too far into my mentoring programs, I discovered the stark reality that if success was to be mine – then it would be up to me to make it happen. And so it is for you. At first the very thought of being in control of my own destiny scared me to death. Now, I wouldn't have it any other way. I cherish the opportunity to call the shots. It's no accident that I found network marketing at the exact right moment when I was ready to expand my horizon beyond the familiar.

Closest to me and those most positively impacted by my networking career are my four precious children ranging in ages from 8 to 25. They top off my list of reasons "WHY?" At first, my greatest driving force was meeting their needs better and providing each of them with the niceties of life. But right behind their names, listed under my reasons "WHY?," are the words 'self discovery' and 'serving others'. I continue to identify new reasons, new seasons, new faces and new places that inspire me to s-t-r-e-t-c-h even further - never losing sight of the four reasons that mattered first and still to this day matter most.

Getting on top of this profession is really not all that difficult. The key is to start where you are and be willing to do it a little wrong, until which time your results tell you and the world that you're doing it right.

Don't allow your mind to tell you, you must do it perfectly, if you are to do it at all. That's the story you create to keep yourself stuck—it probably hasn't served you in the past and certainly will not serve you in your pursuit of excellence here. Step out boldly on to the playing field of free enterprise – suited up for the game. Aggressively gather information and experiences that move you closer and closer to your desired goal. The game is never really over until it's over. That's because new people and new situations will always be coming our way – each prompting us to s-t-r-e-t-c-h yet again.

Here are some tips that have made a big difference in my telltale results…

• Love what you do and love who you do it with
• Work to play
• Determine a perk or reward for you and your loved ones to share in once benchmarks are achieved
• Take an active role in contributing to the success of the company you represent
• Always, even in your leisure time, look and act the part of a successful person until the world sees and experiences you that way and more importantly you see yourself as such
• Early in your career, insulate yourself from nay-sayers
• Appoint yourself a leader and then imitate what other successful leaders are doing
• Form a MasterMind Group made up of individuals with offsetting talents and abilities but equaled in their commitment to bring about a BIG win – fast. (consider including family members in this success mix)
• You and your team must stay connected to the leadership and systems that are proven to work specifically in your business
• Once you've found what works for you, simply do more of the same
• Regularly examine your results to see if any modifications are warranted in your marketing/recruiting/training efforts
• Women…don't let emotions and personalities rule your business. Instead, follow the example of men in our profession who show us how to be excellent designators, goal-setters, comp plan communicators and trouble-shooters extraordinaire
• Men…watch and learn from the women in this industry who model for you what it's like to be a great people connector/relationship builder, and also see and imitate their willingness to begin networking their service/product/money making opportunity to others based on how they feel – BEFORE they know it all.

If I as a high school-educated, technologically-challenged, single mother of four with no advantages to speak of can climb the ladder of success that has put me at the top of this industry – and on top of the world... than you can too... IF you dare to dream and... IF you dare to do.

Janet Larson is a Network Marketing leader and trainer. See www.janetpossible.com or call 480-720-0205.

Race

Minority teens are more interested in starting a business than whites, according to market research firm, Packaged Facts. Also, multi-cultural teens earn more than non-Hispanic White teens.

As of 2004, women of color owned an estimated 1.4 million privately-held firms in the U.S., employing nearly 1.3 million people and generating nearly $147 billion in sales.

Hispanics were the fastest growing minority group between 1982 and 2002. During that same period, American Indians/Alaska Natives were the fastest growing business group.

Age

A 2006 Yahoo poll reports that a growing number of baby boomers feel they will never be too old to launch a business.

The fastest growing age group in direct selling is the 65-year-old and older crowd, reports the Direct Selling Association. As consumers, seniors lay out more than $1.7 trillion per year, making them the richest age group in America.

At the other end of the age spectrum, more college students are considering starting their own business, says the Wall Street Journal. The interest has prompted hundreds of U.S. colleges and universities to offer courses for aspiring entrepreneurs and to help students start their own businesses before graduation.

Geography

Target people by where they live. Examples include:
• Western states in the US has had the highest self-employment rates, 1.8 percent higher than the national average from 1979 to 2003, according to a SBA study.

• Sixty-one inner cities experienced faster small business job growth than their surrounding metropolitan areas from 1995 to 2002. (SBA study)

• From 1985 to 2000, about 55 percent of U.S. sole proprietorships were concentrated in the ten most populous states. Among these ten, Florida was the most nurturing state for sole proprietorship business growth, followed by New York and North Carolina. (SBA study)

For a list of demographic statistical sources, see www.pasbdc.org/what/resources/statistics.asp

Seasons and Special Occasions

Time your marketing to coincide with special occasions. Gift buying peaks in the months leading up to end-of-the- year holidays. Buyers start looking for unique gift ideas as early as September.

Special days like Mother's Day are an ideal time to promote specific product offers. According to a survey by Constant Contact, small business owners report that Mother's Day generates stronger sales than

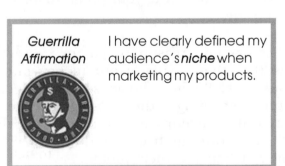

Guerrilla Affirmation — I have clearly defined my audience's *niche* when marketing my products.

Valentine's Day, Easter, Father's Day, and Fourth of July.

More times you can capitalize on include: New Year's resolutions, Easter, spring cleaning, summer vacation, bridal showers, baby showers, anniversary parties, birthdays, open houses, house warmings, Halloween, the Super Bowl, and back to school.

"There are two types of people—those who come into a room and say, 'Well, here I am!' and those who come in and say, 'Ah, there you are.'"
~ Frederick L Collins ~

TACTIC 5. SEEKING BUSINESS-MINDED DISTRIBUTORS

Go for distributors who are entrepreneurial-minded. There's no shortage—around two-thirds of Americans are aspiring entrepreneurs according to a 2006 Yahoo poll. Instead of asking "Who's a prospect?" ask "Who's a prospector?" Seek candidates:
- With a consistent positive outlook
- Who have connections to reach others
- Who show they believe in themselves
- Who have business experience
- Who are decisive and willing to take action
- Who will commit to your program for six months to a year.

A compelling reason to go for entrepreneurial types is that they regularly put money into growing their business. When a business owner looks at an opportunity, she weighs the costs against the potential returns. Entrepreneurs invest money on their own growth and training because they know that the training will improve their profits.

A consumer looks at how much she can afford to pay. She sees putting money out as a cost—one of many she must choose from every day. You can present your comp plan to her all day long, but unless you can shift her buying perspective, she'll continue to perceive your enrollment fee as a consumer choice.

If you hanker after big commission checks, pursue executives, like Doug Firebaugh did.

Looking Where Others Don't
by Doug Firebaugh

The story of my start in Network Marketing is a very interesting one. While I was working out at a gym in 1986, someone gave me a VHS tape to watch. He wanted my input. It was the typical recruiting tactic with nothing special about it.

That was the problem. It carried no impact. Everyone was doing it that way.

I felt deep down inside that there had to be something more powerful that could be done than just going to your friends and family and talking to them. Now do not get this wrong. I believe that you need to talk to friends and family. However, I also believe that there are other ways to do this business as well. As I looked at this industry, I was asking myself one question: "What is no one else doing?" I wanted to go where no one else was going, and do what no one else was doing. I felt that there would be an untapped Gold Mine for this business called Multilevel Marketing within that thought process.

I looked at over thirty different possible starting markets that had few, if any, distributors approaching these markets. During my research, I discovered a market that turned out to be a virtual Gold Mine:

CEOs and Presidents of Corporations.

Sounds nice. They have a lot of prestige and power. But why would we want to start there?

They had three things that most people did not: 1) Most had acquired a large network. 2) Most had credibility with this network. 3) Most had easy access to this network.

Let me see...Large Network? Check! Credibility? Check! Access to this large Network? Check! To me, that spelled "perfect." Now here was the challenge:

How would I get to these CEOs and Presidents, many of whom were totally unapproachable?

I thought about it for a couple of days, and put some ideas down on paper. When I looked at them, none of them really made sense. I thought about it some more, and still, nothing looked like it would be worth pursuing as a possible strategy for striking Gold in my "Hidden Gold Mine" market that I had decided to pursue.

Flustered, I called a friend of my dad's, who had been something of a mentor in my life as he was quite the entrepreneur. I simply was seeking his advice on what to do. The thought had crossed my mind that I desired to start in a place that was too hard to reach.

So I called him.

Mr. Nelson listened intently as I explained what I was looking to do. Then I asked him for any help that he could offer. After all, he was worth millions and had a lot of experience and wisdom.

He was silent for a moment, and then quietly said, "Your answer lies within the beginning of this call." I thought I had heard him correctly, but had no clue about what he was talking about. So I asked Mr. Nelson if he could explain what he just said.

"Sure" he said. "When you called me, you said that you were doing some research looking for different ways to approach this professional market. You were searching for some experienced wisdom and advice. You said that you were starting a business, and that you were where I once was forty years ago — at the very beginning of the journey. You asked if I could offer you some advice about how to succeed. And you asked what I did at the start of my business. You asked if we could meet for lunch. Is that not true?"

"Yes," I replied.

"There is your answer. Do not try to do business with these CEOs and Presidents right off the bat. Odds are, they are too busy. But one thing most successful people are NOT too busy to do is to help other aspiring young entrepreneurs. Most will take the time, or even a lunch, to help and encourage people who are willing to go beyond just the run of a mill life. That is my suggestion."

"Mr. Nelson, may I ask one more question?" I inquired.

"Sure," he said as he smiled.

"How is the best way to approach them?"

"Send a letter of introduction, and ask to interview them over lunch. Call their secretaries as well to schedule the meeting. Be grateful and humble, and have a ten question interview sheet that you use with every CEO. Once you have taken one CEO to lunch, ask him or her to recommend someone else with whom you could talk. This question will prove to be worth your time. They probably will have someone in mind. Start with this question: When did you decide that you were going to be a CEO of a company and why did you decide that? Is there anything else? I have a meeting to attend."

"When may I take you to lunch?" I asked.

Laughing, he told me to call his secretary and schedule it.

We did exactly what Mr. Nelson said to do. We sent the CEOs and Presidents an introduction letter and asked if we could interview them over lunch. Some said no, but most said yes. Some had us come to their offices. We played by their rules and not ours. Let me be clear about something. We had no intentions of recruiting them or trying to sell them anything. Our focus was to take advantage of their wisdom and to get some of their million-dollar advice. Yes, they had contacts, and yes, we would appreciate an introduction to someone they might know. Many did just that. We simply followed the format during each interview on the ten question sheet which turned into a Gold Mine of information.

Did we recruit any of them? Absolutely. Did we move a lot of product? You bet.

How?

By asking one final question on the sheet. "Do you have a rolodex? What percentage of that list of names is currently producing you any kind of revenue? 5 percent? 10 percent? Would you like to turn that into 30 percent or maybe higher?"

As they say, the rest is history. Our Success was blessed beyond measure, and all of it started with the million-dollar question, "What are people NOT doing that is something worth doing?"

Do not think outside of the box. Burn the box with the Fire of Unlimited Imagination and Boundless Passion. As Mr. Nelson always said, "Thinking outside of the box is for those individuals who only want a bigger box. Get rid of it! Let your incredible imagination be unleashed upon an unsuspecting world."

Doug Firebaugh is an in-demand speaker, trainer, author and entrepreneur. He has helped over 10,000 people reach an annual income of more than $50,000 a year. See www.passionfire.com.

12 Ways to Reach Your Audience

Maximize your marketing's results by targeting appropriate audiences by what's important to them. Invest your resources wisely, instead of indiscriminate advertising, hoping to reach everyone. Here are twelve ways to get your message to your target prospects, including:

1. Identify publications they read
2. Find associations they belong to
3. Discover websites they visit
4. Join discussion groups they participate in
5. Read magazines and newsletters they subscribe to
6. Get involved with what they do
7. Visit stores they buy specific supplies from
8. Attend trade shows they go to

9. Study their industry

10. Watch TV shows they watch

11. Learn who are the movers and shakers

12. Build relationships with the industry leaders

For example, say that you are a direct sales rep for a craft related party plan and you are seeking leads. There are lots of craft magazines and websites crafters rely on for tips and ideas—check out the magazine area at your bookstore. Crafters buy supplies from more than 15,000 craft supply stores around the US—some have bulletin boards; crafters watch cable TV programs—inquire how to get invited as a featured guest; and crafters like to join clubs and guilds related to their craft to network with others.

"You can make more friends in two months by becoming interested in other people than you can in two years by trying to get other people interested in you."
~ Dale Carnegie ~

Niche marketing saves money because you only invest resources in getting your message to people most likely to purchase your product. Without niche marketing:

1. Customers cannot differentiate your offer from any others, which leads to lower perceived value of your product at best and, more often, just being ignored.

2. You won't know who your customers are. Your marketing efforts are like a hunter, closing his eyes and firing a shotgun into the air, hoping to hit something.

3. You will miss opportunities. By focusing your marketing toward a niche audience, you will learn about your audience's specific problems and uncover

solutions that will lead to discovering new or related products to ease their pain.

Listen to your audience and it will tell you what products and services to offer it.

Checklist for this Chapter's Tactics

Place a check in the appropriate column for determining how or if you will use a tactic. Then return to your 7-sentence marketing plan - see Chapter 3 - and fill in the appropriate tactics in Step 4 of your plan.

Tactics In This Chapter	Using Well	Using, But Needs Work	Not Using	Not Right At This Time
4. Identifying Niche Audiences				
5. Seeking Business-Minded Prospects				

"He who every morning plans the transaction of the day and follows out that plan, carries a thread that will guide him through the maze of the most busy life. But where no plan is laid, where the disposal of time is surrendered merely to the chance of incidence, chaos will soon reign."

~ Victor Hugo ~

CHAPTER 5

Tactics About You

"Of all the things that can have an effect on your future, I believe personal growth is the greatest. We can talk about sales growth, profit growth, asset growth, but all of this probably will not happen without personal growth."
~ Jim Rohn ~

The successful network marketer lives in the center of an ever growing circle of distributors and customers. She or he attracts people seemingly out of the blue. But there is a reason people are drawn to them. Top earners become magnetic by tapping into their existing resources—resources also at your command right now.

As you learn more tactical ways to get your offer out there, remember that people must buy *you*, before they commit to your program. This chapter covers six important ways to help you make the most out of *you* as a marketing tactic:

1. Your passion
2. Your personal growth
3. Your positive attitude
4. Your network
5. Your product knowledge
6. Your market knowledge

TACTIC 6. YOUR PASSION

When you are on fire about what you have, you can barely contain yourself from telling the world. Without it, you probably won't say much.

Passion is a powerful persuader—more motivating than logic. Eighty percent of our decisions are made from emotion. Studies reveal that only after we have made an emotional choice, do we then go back and justify it with reason.

Excitement is contagious. Beyond words, it convinces others that the product or offer we're excited about delivers real value.

Enthusiasm sparks word-of-mouth referrals. But, it can be a challenge to stay totally enthused all day, every day. When you feel your eagerness waning, look to these nine areas in network marketing for more inspiration:

1. Love for your product
2. Desire to help people
3. Enthusiasm for your parent company
4. Excitement for the compensation plan
5. Bonding with your sponsor
6. Being part of a community or team
7. Fervor for marketing
8. Passion to grow and learn
9. Eagerness to enjoy time-freedom

"What is it that you like doing? If you don't like it, get out of it, because you'll be lousy at it. You don't have to stay with a job for the rest of your life, because if you don't like it you'll never be successful in it."
~ Lee Iacocca ~

TACTIC 7. YOUR PERSONAL GROWTH

Studies show personal growth plays an important role in success. Although it's called "personal" growth, it often shows itself in how we deal with others. Carnegie Mellon University and Stanford Research Institute did a study showing that job success relies 75 percent on skills working with people but only 25 percent of success came from technical skills.

Growth means something different to everyone. It may refer to bettering relationships, improving health and fitness, embracing natural medicine, cultivating inner awareness, recovering from alcohol or drugs, spiritual faith, or all of these.

Whatever the specific area in life, the common denominator is the desire to improve oneself. Many successful people cite personal growth as the number one factor contributing to their achievement.

Maintaining an attitude of growing and improving helps you get up again after you fall, allows you to forgive your own and other's mistakes, and feeds your soul with hope for a better future.

Positive-thinking books, tapes, and seminars have long been tools for learning in network marketing. Any vehicle for positive change will do, as long as your intention is to find and move toward your next level of improvement.

Personal improvement carries over into your marketing results. Exercising and eating healthy improves your looks. Studies show people make eleven assumptions about you based on your appearance.

How you dress influences your prospect's choice to do business with you. Your prospect assumes that your neatness or lack of it is a reflection of how you will treat them.

Adopting good habits will increase your attraction factor, make you feel better, and give you more energy. Your energy, appearance and vitality infuse everything you do with contagious excitement. People long for the success your life is an example of.

"I'm a big believer in growth. Life is not about achievement, it's about learning and growth, and developing qualities like compassion, patience, perseverance, love, and joy, and so forth. And so if that is the case, then I think our goals should include something which stretches us."
~ Jack Canfield ~

Since your marketing emanates from *you*, you'll maximize the results from all your other efforts by continually upgrading *you*. Dress up, care for, and support the source from which all your communications and activities issue.

Tactic 8. Your Positive Attitude

One of the biggest contributors to personal growth is your attitude. The way you think will be either your greatest ally or your worst enemy. Harvard University conducted a study which reported that 85 percent of getting a job or a promotion came from the applicant's attitude.

First impressions last longest, so make your initial communications positive ones that will continue to work for you later. People like people who radiate positive feelings.

One positive thought leads to another positive thought. One negative thought leads to another negative thought. According to a Stanford Research Institute study, nearly 90 percent of our inner mental chatter is negative so you have to make efforts to discard them and get your mind on something positive.

If you are having trouble getting positive, make more friends. After studying people with depression, researchers in the UK reported that friendships help make you and your friends feel important, respected, and cared about—all of which contribute to a positive attitude and a larger network.

TACTIC 9. YOUR NETWORK

Conventional network marketing says start your business by approaching people you know—your warm list. In many cases, people you know are more inclined to help you and more forgiving of your mistakes.

David Teten and Scott Allen, authors of *"How to Use Online Networks to Market Your Business,"* report that more than 40 percent of people in the U.S. seek the advice of friends and family when looking for services. Other studies agree that word of mouth among friends may be the most effective way businesses get referrals.

The average person knows around 100 to 200 or more people. If you can't recall many names, go through the following list and use these memory joggers to compile a list of people in your network:

• Friends - present and previous co-workers, went to school together, live nearby or did, served in the military together, met online through a social networking or online dating site

• Family - parents and grandparents, siblings, cousins, aunts and uncles, children and grandchildren, nieces and nephews, in-laws

---

*"It is your attitude, not your aptitude,
that determines your altitude."*
~ Zig Ziglar ~

• Fitness - golf, running, biking, baseball, football, basketball, swimming, martial arts, lifting weights, fitness trainer, bowling, tennis, dance partner, dance instructor

• Community - church, neighborhood association events, lodge meetings like Rotary or Lion's Club, political meetings, police officer

• School - school events, teachers or administrators, coaches, PTAs, parents of your kid's friends, babysitter, school crossing guard

• Casual - grocery store, mall, bus stop, waiting for your car at the carwash, while doing laundry, walking your dog, bars and night clubs, waiting at airports, bus and train stations, sitting next to them on planes, buses and trains, meeting them on a cruise or other vacation, taxi or bus driver, janitor

• Caretakers - doctor, chiropractor, veterinarian, dentist, dental hygienist, eye doctor, nurse, pharmacist, herbalist, massage therapist, psychologist, physical therapist, occupational therapist, nutritionist, personal coach, acupuncturist, receptionist

• Daily business - check out clerk, housecleaner, waiter or waitress, hair stylist, barber, manicurist, appliance repair person, handyman, bank clerk, postal clerk, postal delivery person, convenience store clerk, landlord, travel agent, mechanic, daycare manager, florist, dry cleaner, plumber, electrician, garbage collector, lawn care, gardener, landscaper

• Professional - accountant, lawyer, realtor, mortgage broker, notary public, banker, financial planner, insurance agent, business owner, store manager, engineer, architect, home builder, artist,

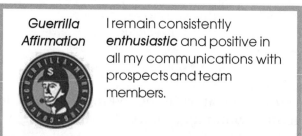

Guerrilla Affirmation I remain consistently *enthusiastic* and positive in all my communications with prospects and team members.

musician, graphic designer, interior decorator, computer programmer.

Even people in your network only vaguely connected to you can turn into business leaders, like with John David Mann.

The Power of Fuzzy: You Have the Most Influence on People You Know . . . Vaguely
by John David Mann

Where will you find your strongest leaders for your network marketing business? The good old tried-'n'-true MCI "friends and family"? Or that dreaded beast, the "cold market"?

Actually, the answer may surprise you: neither one. The chances are excellent that you'll find your best leaders among those people you already know . . . *sort of.*

Prospects come from three domains: (1) your inner circle, or "warm market"; (2) the world at large, or "cold market"; or (3) the fuzzy area in between—and that last is the most fruitful by far. It includes all those people you know *vaguely*—not exactly friends, but not exactly strangers, either—the teller at your bank, your kids' friends' moms, a distant classmate from college years ago. People whose faces you know, if not their names. Friends of friends of friends. We don't have a term for this not-warm-but-not-cold-either realm, and that's too bad. Because that's where you'll find the overwhelming majority of successful network-building partners.

Let's call them the "fuzzy market." And the amazing thing is that the fuzzy market is where your leaders will most likely come from.

Really? Yes, really! Who says? Science—and experience.

First, I'll give you some science to back me up. And then I'll give you something better: a story.

First: what about friends and family? It happens, but rather more rarely. Complete strangers, from an ad or lead generation system, or people one simply meets on the street, on a plane, on a train? (Imagine *Strangers on a Train* if Hitchcock had been a network marketer: "I know . . . I'll prospect *your* warm list, and you prospect *mine*! Criss-cross!") Again, it happens. But 90 percent or more of the successful network marketers I've ever seen have been people whose sponsors knew them, but only vaguely, before they joined the network.

Malcolm Gladwell, a staff writer for *The New Yorker*, confirms this observation in his best-selling book about influence, *The Tipping Point*. Gladwell describes a classic 1974 study in which sociologist Mark Granovetter looked at several hundred professional and technical workers from Newton, Massachusetts to find out how they found their current jobs. More than half learned about their positions through personal contacts. This was no big surprise, but the next part was: of those who used a personal contact to find a job, only 16 percent saw that contact *often* (i.e., close friends), and more than 55 percent saw that contact only *occasionally*.

According to Granovetter, you are far less likely to learn about a new opportunity through a close friend because your friends occupy the same world you do. You are far more likely to learn about something new from someone you know only vaguely. He calls it "the strength of weak ties," and concludes that those with whom you share only weak ties represent far more social power than your close friends.

Look at it from the other direction: with what people do you hold the power of weak ties? On whom do you have the most influence? Your siblings? Ha! They were there when you were wetting the bed. (You approach your older brother with, "Do you keep your financial options open?" and he grunts, "Yeah, why, Squirt, you starting a company that sells waterproof pajamas?") From complete strangers? Maybe, in time . . . but you'll have to earn it from scratch. But acquaintances? That's where you already have power: the power of weak ties. Your *fuzzy* market.

A few years ago, I got an e-mail from a woman named Amy. I went to high school with Amy. To tell the truth, we weren't close friends; in fact, we hardly knew each other. But I'd started this alternative high school (yes, I *started* it—you can read more about it in my book, *The Zen of MLM*), and Amy was a student there. I was not good at staying in touch with my high school friends. But thirty years later, I got an e-mail from her—and I thought she and my sweetheart Ana would get along like a house on fire. So I put them together, and they did.

That was two years ago. Last month, I threw a surprise party for Ana I (now my fiancée) and, completely unbeknownst to her, flew in her two best friends in the world to meet her at our favorite restaurant. One of those two best friends in the world—you guessed it—was Amy.

Yes, Amy and Ana hit it off—and not only did they hit it off, but Amy also became one of Ana's strongest leaders in her burgeoning network marketing organization. Today Ana is earning a high six figures per year, a sizeable chunk of which comes from Amy's organization.

Did Amy *know* Ana? No. Was she a stranger? No. She knew *me* . . . sort of. She was fuzzy.

Go for fuzzy. It's where you'll find your fortune, and your future.

John David Mann is author of The Zen of MLM *(www.zenofmlm.com) and coauthor of* The Go-Giver *(www.thego-giver.com).*

People prefer working with those they know and like. But use common sense when communicating to people in your network about your product or opportunity. Learn if someone is seeking solutions like you provide before offering them. Avoid treating family or friends like sales targets. Talk to people who are close to you face-to-face, rather than sending impersonal sales material.

Eventually, your warm list runs out. The guerrilla tactics in this book will help you attract streams of new prospects and learn ways to transform those prospects into new friends, and then into life-long customers, or successful business builders. Those people will all have networks, too.

Tactic 10. Your Product Knowledge

When a prospect asks a question about your offer, be able to talk about your own experiences in terms of benefits which relate directly to the other person's situation.

List all the benefits you and other customers have experienced from your marketing plan in Chapter 3. Keep your list on hand and go over it regularly to rekindle your enthusiasm and to keep those benefits fresh in your mind.

Explore all your company's products. Experience is the best form of knowledge. The guerrilla network marketer has lots of product knowledge and experiences and is always ready to share these stories with others at appropriate moments. Check out products like yours reviewed in newsletters, magazines, online, TV or anywhere else that can give you more useful information about your own items.

Come up with a list of product usage tips that make a 'tip sheet' you can give to customers and team members. The more you know about your product, the more trust your prospects will feel, which converts to higher sales.

Remember that your business opportunity is a product, too. Being able to answer questions about your compensation plan instills trust. See Chapter 19 for more on how to use your comp plan as a tactic.

"People are definitely a company's greatest asset. It doesn't make any difference whether the product is cars or cosmetics. A company is only as good as the people it keeps."
~ Mary Kay Ash ~

TACTIC 11. YOUR MARKET KNOWLEDGE

Perhaps even more strategic than product knowledge, is knowing and understanding your market. The more informed you are about trends, statistics, and facts, the more credible you will come across as a helpful resource.

For instance, when promoting your travel service, you should know the average amount of time and money a consumer takes when booking travel, so you can show him how to save. If you are promoting a natural skin care line, you should have statistics on how much of a health risk all the chemicals commonly found in commercial beauty products causes.

"Suppliers and especially manufacturers have market power because they have information about a product or a service that the customer does not and cannot have."
~ Peter Drucker ~

Gather 5 to 10 riveting true facts about the market related to your product or service industry (not your MLM company) and know them well enough that you can confidently mention them in a face-to-face meeting. Include them on your website and in your marketing materials.

Examples of market knowledge include:

• In the last 50 years, 80,000 new chemicals have been created and the majority of them have not been tested for long-term impact according to www.ToxicNation.com. *Can you use this when marketing natural household cleaner?*

• In 2005, airline flights from New York to Fort Lauderdale topped the list of destinations with 4,160,000 flights (U.S. Census.) *Selling vacation packages in Florida?*

• The average person consumed 56.9 pounds of fats and oils in 1980. By 2004, consumption was up to 87.5 pounds. *Good for weight loss info.*

• In 1980, the average person drank 33.6 gallons of soft drinks; by 2004, we were downing 52.3 gallons (U.S. Census.) *With all that carbonated beverage, you can bet we need more digestive enzymes.*

• Are baby boomers feeling crunched for more income? Yes, according to the Administrative Office of US Courts, boomers over 55 years old are filing for bankruptcy at a faster rate than the general population due in part to increasing reliance on debt. *Does this tell you boomers make good prospects for your opportunity? You bet.*

The more you know about your market, the more you position yourself as a true expert. Who do you think people will choose to do business with, a person who is trying to *sell* or a person who can confidently educate and help?

Ready to learn how to find market data on your product or industry? Visit www.knowthis.com and click on the link to tutorials and then follow the link to Market Research.

Guerrilla Affirmation

When listening on the phone, I will take notes with details about the other person. I can then use my notes as a jumping off place to begin my next follow-up communication with the person.

Checklist for this Chapter's Tactics

Place a check in the appropriate column for determining how or if you will use a tactic. Then return to your 7-sentence marketing plan - see Chapter 3 - and fill in the appropriate tactics in Step 4 of your plan.

Tactics In This Chapter	Using Well	Using, But Needs Work	Not Using	Not Right At This Time
6. Your Passion				
7. Your Personal Growth				
8. Your Positive Attitude				
9. Your Network				
10. Your Product Knowledge				
11. Your Market Knowledge				

CHAPTER 6

TACTICS ABOUT PEOPLE

---

*"All things being equal, people buy
from friends. All things NOT being
equal, people buy from friends."*
~ Jeffrey Gitomer, author of *The Sales Bible* ~

The important thing to remember about people is they prefer doing business with those they like. One of the ways to get others to like you is to create rapport. The word rapport is derived from a French word, *rapporter*, meaning "to bring back." To grow sales month after month, bring people back again and again. Rapport gives people reasons to like you, to choose to come back.

This chapter helps you get people to like you through six important ways to build rapport:
1. Smiles and greetings
2. Body language
3. Active listening
4. Identifying people's core needs
5. Linking your network to the world
6. Using stories

TACTIC 12. SMILES AND GREETINGS

A smile initiates an immediate human bond, a bond that exceeds any mere business offer. When you smile, you are telling people they are special. Smile frequently because it costs you nothing, generates tons of goodwill, and sets the mood for friendship. People like to do business with people who are happy. One guerrilla put it this way, "A smile is the shortest distance between two people."

Here's a tip for making your greeting memorable. As soon as you can after meeting someone, repeat the person's name back to him. People like people who remember them. It's one of the simplest ways to elevate your importance in another person's mind.

"A smile is a powerful weapon;
you can even break ice with it."
~ Anonymous ~

When Greeting People by Phone

• Answer your phone the same way every time
• Respond to the caller's questions clearly and honestly
• Be courteous, even when the caller isn't
• Understand that your time is important (don't linger on with conversations)
• Smile while talking on the phone, because the receiving person can sense when you are genuinely pleased to be speaking.

TACTIC 13. BODY LANGUAGE

According to MSNBC's Today, 65 percent to 90 percent of every conversation is interpreted through body language. When a person sees you, they form an unconscious assessment of you from your body language, which studies show influences them as much as seven times more than the words you use.

You can put someone at ease very quickly through mirroring the person's body language and voice patterns.

Guerrilla Affirmation

I remember to dress a little better than those I meet with face to face. My appearance speaks volumes about my success so I make sure it sends the right message.

You may already have noticed yourself doing this naturally while speaking with a friend. People like people who are like them.

When meeting with someone for the first time, observe the person's postures and gestures. If the person is sitting straight up or standing and leaning slightly, very gradually match his stance. If the person is crossing his legs, cross yours. You can increase rapport by matching the tone, pace, and pitch of his voice with your own.

The idea of mirroring is not to manipulate the other person, but to get in sync with him, to enter his world.

The tricky part of matching body language or voice tone and pitch with someone you don't know is that if you move too fast to copy the other person, he may interpret it as a contrived device, which will create a block to rapport. The key to effective matching is to make the adjustments slowly, naturally, and without obvious intention.

Women are better at interpreting body language then men. Women naturally read others feelings because they have the innate ability to pick up subtle shifts in another person's voice and body language, according to Dr. David Geary, psychology professor at the University of Missouri.

TACTIC 14. ACTIVE LISTENING

People like people who listen to them. Listen actively to people and they will tell you exactly what will help them. You won't have to guess. You won't have to rely on sales techniques. You'll know what to do, because they will tell you.

The problem is that most people don't know how to listen. Often when people speak to each other face-to-face, they only partially listen. Their thoughts are about something that happened in the past or something they think is going to happen in the future. Active listening means that you are completely present with the person you're engage with; listening beyond words for meaning.

Active listening differs from typical listening in that your attention is intentionally focused on the other person, not just politely giving him time while you are thinking about your response.

The test is if, after the other person has spoken, you can repeat back the essential message. If so, then you were consciously present. You paid attention and understood the other person.

"Listening is a magnetic and strange thing, a creative force. The friends who listen to us are the ones we move toward. When we are listened to, it creates us, makes us unfold and expand."
~ Brenda Ueland ~

Learn to use active listening whenever speaking with prospects, whenever talking with existing customers, and whenever communicating with your downline team.

By developing a habit of active listening, you can get people to have a more open attitude toward you. You can avoid miscommunications. You can clear up conflicts. Perhaps most importantly, you can build trust and confidence.

Tips for listening with intention include:

• Cease any interfering activities before the conversation.

• If you are in a restaurant or other place with frequent traffic, avoid looking at passersby.

• Turn off your cell phone.

• If the person is someone you know, remark on a point of how a recent previous conversation went and concluded.

• If you made notes about the person, look over them ahead of the new meeting.

• Be aware of any emotions you may have and put them aside.

• Suspend your opinions or judgments.

• Focus your attention toward hearing the person's words.

• Be aware that your intention is to learn what the other person has to say, not to talk about yourself.

• Don't interrupt a person's comments.

• When asked a question, answer briefly.

• When the person finishes talking, pause a moment before speaking.

• In your own words, repeat the important points or a summary to affirm your understanding of the situation.

• Ask questions to clarify points.

By actively listening, you can discover critical information, learn if you can truly help, and then wisely choose how much energy to invest in someone.

> *"If you want to win friends, make it a point to remember them. If you remember my name, you pay me a subtle compliment; you indicate that I have made an impression on you. Remember my name and you add to my feeling of importance."*
> ~ Dale Carnegie ~

TACTIC 15. IDENTIFYING CORE NEEDS

Experts differ in how human needs are named and prioritized, yet common denominators appear in all the lists. Our core human requirements can be summarized as:

- Safety - security - feeling protected
- Love - connection - a sense of belonging
- Self-esteem - significance - to be respected
- Diversity - challenge - creative expression
- Growth - self actualization - ability to control
- Contribution - peak experiences - transcendence

When deciding to buy a product or commit to an action, each person is asking himself, "What's in it for me?" People don't care about your goal to make Diamond level by the end of the month. They care about how to solve their own problems and create a better life.

Before you can know if you can help someone, you must take the time to discover the person's individual requirements. Your prospects will come to you with different challenges.

If you neglect to learn an individual's situation, you come across like the typical salesperson who doggedly repeats the same presentation to everyone, over and over again. A ritual presentation will result in a small percentage of people buying, but it will cost you more over time, because you must make many more rote performances just to get new customers. As fast as you *sell* new people in, previous buyers are on their way out.

Increase your long-term results by acknowledging each person you communicate with. Learn what's going on with someone by actively listening when the person is talking and by asking questions.

Sample questions to learn the requirements of a prospective distributor:

- What is missing in your life to keep you from being successful?
- What keeps you tied to your situation?
- What are your challenges with your current income?
- What is becoming harder to achieve?
- What is your vision for your future?
- When will you achieve the lifestyle you choose to have?
- What is your greatest challenge?
- What concerns would prevent you from getting started now?
- What worries you?
- What can I do to help you?

Sample questions to learn the requirements of a prospective customer:

- What problems are you experiencing?
- Where do you buy your _____? (Currently used product related to yours.)
- What problems is the product you use now failing to solve?
- What factors influence your choice to buy?

- Do you do any research before you make a purchase?
- What product have you not yet found that would help solve a problem in your life?
- What can I do to help you?

A frequently asked question in network marketing is, "should I lead with the business opportunity or the product?" If you would have more of both loyal customers and active distributors, invest time getting to know your prospects before assuming that leading one way or another will fit every situation.

"A person who seems to have all the answers usually isn't listening."
~ Jeffrey Gitomer ~

Network marketing is a people-business and every person has different challenges. People are not interested in your product or your business; they are interested in solving their own problems.

Tactic 16. Linking Your Network to the World

International sponsoring can be a lucrative part of your marketing campaign. More than eighty percent of direct selling companies operate internationally. Direct sales revenues in Asia ($36.5 billion) exceeds sales in North America ($34.7 billion) according to the Direct Selling Association.

Every culture has nuances of etiquette that influence successful communications. Guerrillas exploit the advantages of communicating according to specific cultures.

Be sure your organization and income is solid locally before setting your sights internationally, reports Kosta Gara.

Your People: Your Key to Global Expansion
by Kosta Gara

As I write this piece, I am enjoying a wonderfully sunny day on the Vancouver coast. I am fully refreshed having just returned from a month-long European vacation that took me to ten different countries. It was a dream vacation. We dined in the best restaurants, stayed in the swankiest hotels, and shopped in some of Europe's trendiest stores and districts.

Sitting around my pool, I cannot help but reflect on how I have achieved so much having just turned thirty-five years of age. My life today is so completely different than the one I endured when my mother made the difficult decision to leave our homeland.

We came from a war-torn part of the world that held little hope for the future. But simply leaving was illegal. We had to escape. Escape meant paying exorbitant fees to unscrupulous people-smugglers. It meant climbing treacherous mountain passes and crossing open water in overcrowded rubber rafts. We literally risked our lives to make it to Canada.

But we made it. I still recall my arrival as a small boy. In my broken English, I asked our cab driver "What's the best thing about Canada?" He answered "Canada is a land of opportunities, son." His words still resonate with me today.

Opportunities indeed! Today, I lead an organization that spans five continents and over forty countries with more than 175,000 distributors. It is the third largest network in the entire network marketing industry in Canada. And I achieved all of this in six short years.

How did I achieve all of this? I built an organization that focused on recruiting, empowering, and building leaders. I shared my philosophy, work ethic, and never-ending optimism with all of them. My goal was to teach them to succeed so that they could pass on what they learned to others.

Most importantly, I did not rush the growth process. I developed a methodical plan that would enable me to build a solid international presence. I did not want my organization to crumble in the face of a strong breeze. Let me tell you about my plan.

International expansion was vital to the success I enjoy today. It is also doomed to failure if not properly executed. Expanding before you are truly ready will leave you unprepared. And preparation is essential.

It may sound ironic, but I prepared for my international growth by focusing at the local level. By local, I mean that I recruited people who already lived in my area code. These were people with whom I had the greatest level of credibility. I could easily explain to them how my methods would allow them to also achieve their own goals and dreams. When they began to taste the success of my methods, they could not help but spread the word amongst their contacts. Then, I simply allowed the principle of "six degrees of separation" to take over.

Some of you may be familiar with this principle. It implies that we are all just six people away from each person on the planet. Every new contact you make has the potential to bring someone to your network that resides outside of your area code. That person is your key to unlocking the door to expansion. When your existing local network is sufficiently well established, you can then duplicate your systems in the new area. Gradually, your organization can become national in scope. International expansion is then an almost unavoidable step.

Be prepared for challenges. Barriers such as language and cultural differences will arise. Overseas expansion is costly. That is why it should only be undertaken when your local and national networks are firmly established. When you are ready, begin by developing leaders overseas who can implement your systems for you. They will train others to succeed as you have trained them. Let them develop the critical mass of people you need to justify the expense of traveling to these destinations.

Make sure your international expansion begins with people who can speak English as well as the local language. These people are vital to your ability to communicate. Keep in mind that some people will be able to understand some English if you speak slowly. Slow down your speech. Allow them to follow you.

When conducting business overseas, it is imperative that you respect the culture of the host country or you risk offending them. Take the time to learn about the culture before you go.

For instance, in Korea, people stop working at 6p.m. Evenings are dedicated to family. That is their way and you have to accept it, even though in North America the network marketers are just beginning to work at that time. If I had tried to force my views upon my Korean distributors, I never would have succeeded in my efforts to grow there. I planned my activities around their practices. Today, some of our best distributors are in Korea.

I cannot think of another industry that would allow me to experience so much at such a young age. Where else could I have the freedom to truly set my own agenda. I am free to travel and experience so many new cultures. I have amazing friends all over the world. It is a dream life. Coming from the life of hardship and poverty I once experienced, I cannot believe my life has become so radically different. I know that if I can do it, so can you.

At age thirty-one, Kosta Gara, network marketing trainer, distributor and MLM consultant became the youngest million-dollar annual earner in his company. He is the co-author of More Build It Big *and has been featured in* Networking Times *magazine. See* www.kostagara.com.

The more you understand a culture's etiquette, the more respect you will get from the natives and the faster they will accept and bond with you.

In the United Kingdom, it is prevalent to use first names when communicating, but only after you are invited to. Germans make appointments for most things and are punctual down to the minute; don't be early or late. In Japan, it is difficult to get appointments with strangers unless you mention a mutual connection with a person who referred you.

For more insights into appropriate ways to communicate and market internationally, see www.executiveplanet.com and www.cyborlink.com.

Speaking People's Language

People like people who speak their language. While you listen to someone to discover what's going on in his life, the next step is to understand how he communicates, in order for you get on his wavelength.

According to Dr. Duane Lakin, Ph.D., author of *The Unfair Advantage*, almost everyone you come into contact with will communicate in language that indicates a preference for one of three senses: vision, hearing, or touch. You can build a bond with people by knowing which sense faculty is dominate and by using words aligned with that sense in your communications. For example, a visually-dominate person may *see* how to make a choice. An auditory person will *hear* how it sounds. A kinesthetic person *feels* the solution.

By paying attention to the words someone uses in conversation, you can quickly learn which sense dominates.

Guerrilla Affirmation

I ask my customers, prospects, and downline team members about their needs and *actively listen* to their answers.

A visually-dominant person may use such words as "I can't see myself quitting my job," or "I don't know what that would look like." This person will *visualize* an idea. You must *paint a picture* or *show* him.

An auditory person uses words such words as "I hear you on that," or "Let me talk to my husband." Here, your communication must *sound good* or *loud and clear*. It must *ring true*.

The kinesthetic person has to "get a feel for it" or is more comfortable with "a solid base" or "a concrete idea." This is a person who will *go* for your product, but needs to know the *impact* it will have on his or her life. You must make a *connection* with this person.

Pay attention to the words your prospects use and speak in their language. The faster you do this, the sooner they will feel at ease with you and your message. If you fail to match your language to your individual prospects, you risk alienating them; they will not understand the benefits of your offer because you have chosen words to which they don't typically relate.

Speaking to people according to their dominant sensory language is called *pacing,* and it's a proven way to establish trust and rapport, according to NLP (neurolinguistic programming).

TACTIC 17. USING STORIES

People like people who are interesting, people they can relate to as being like themselves. Stories help us link up with others as human beings, sharing experiences.

The most compelling stories are those that evoke strong feelings. Dale Carnegie recommended beginning any speaking presentation with a personal story about an event which holds meaning for you as a quick way to make a connection with your audience.

A fast way to start the bonding process with someone is to actively listen to the person and when it's your turn to speak, tell a story that ties into a point made by the other person.

"Talk to me and I hear;
Show me and I understand;
Tell me a story and I'll remember."
~ Saying ~

It's okay to tell people a story about your network marketing experiences. A study by Northeastern University revealed that letting a prospect know about one's commercial affiliation with a brand had no measurable effect on the credibility of the word-of-mouth message. Over 75 percent of those surveyed relayed that affiliation was a "non-issue." In fact, the survey discovered people who knew of a representative's commercial affiliation were more likely to feel positively about both the representative and the company.

Stories Sell, Facts Just Tell
by Bill Hyman

Ever listen to a really great speaker? Did you notice it's the stories that capture your attention? It's the stories you remember. Stories are good for anchoring your message in your prospect's memory. Studies show that well-told stories increase a person's recall by 26 percent. I remember the story of how I first got involved in Network Marketing like it was yesterday.

When I was a boy, when my Dad asked me what I wanted to be when I grew up. I answered, "I don't know Dad, but I think I would like to be a professional bum." As I reflect back, this may have been a 12-year-old's clumsy definition of MLM success: time freedom and the money to enjoy it.

I dropped out of high school at the end of my junior year. I knew there was more to life than school for me so I decided to visit Europe and the Mideast for a few months. Two and a half years later, I was still in Europe working one odd job after another. A job, even a good paying one was fine, but I knew I wanted to be self-employed.

I moved back to the US and without knowing the first thing about cars, I enrolled in the Milwaukee Area Technical College to learn how to become a Car Mechanic. The idea was simple. Learn enough about cars to some day open my own shop and therefore keep my hands clean and more importantly, be my own boss. After working on cars for six years, I discovered something about myself, I hated working on cars.

Just about that time, I received a phone call from one of my customers. The moment the phone rang, I had a funny feeling. Like whoever this was, it was going to be good news. He started telling me about Network Marketing. So there I was, thinking this is it, my ticket out. I can be self-employed and I can help people, which spoke to the social worker in me. And, I can make money without working on cars.

Truth is MLM is hard work. Maybe harder than anything you have ever done before. The first 18 months in Network Marketing, it seemed I couldn't do anything right. I failed and failed and failed. You might say, I failed my way to the top. A year and a half into the program and still nothing had happened. Despite a strong belief in MLM, it just wasn't working for me.

The thing was, I didn't have a fall back position. I didn't have a degree or a career that could be my safety net. What I had was passion and desire. And I was persistent; I kept learning and searching.

I remember being so determined that I would not fail that I put a large piece of paper on my fridge in the biggest words that would fit: I MAKE NO PROVISIONS FOR FAILURE.

In that first 18 months, I could not find a single leader. Then I found a couple that wanted success as much as I did. That year, I earned $65,000. In the following 18 months, I broke out 35 more leaders.

A few years later, my earnings were in the millions. Today, my MLM business spans the globe, with more than 200,000 distributors.

Network Marketing can set you free; freer than you ever dreamed possible. Free to work with the people you want to work with. Free to live where you want to live in whatever season you want to live there. Freedom from financial worries. Freedom from traffic jams, bosses, memos. Sounds like a dream doesn't it?

To know that I only need to bring my laptop, and with a telephone, I can be in business from anywhere in the world is priceless. To appreciate the ability to say to myself, "It is gorgeous outside today. I'm not going to work." Sure, I didn't arrive at this level of freedom overnight. It took a lot of trial and error. But the rewards have been worth it.

Bill's rule number one. Find a company that you can be off the charts passionate about. Make sure they are planning for long term and there is good growth potential.

Rule number two. Be Coach-Able. The successful people in your upline have a system that you should follow. Don't reinvent the wheel, you will only frustrate yourself.

Rule number three. Develop *your* story, not just the one about your background and why you decided to join, which is very important, but also your success. Your first span of time (several months) often determines your future successes. So work as hard in the beginning as you possibly can. Remember, success breeds success and if you get off to a fast start, you can ride that success to the next level.

Rule number four. Once the above are in place, don't look back for at least 18 months. It's your attitude not your aptitude that determines your altitude. If you have a "whatever it takes" attitude, that does not allow you to quit, it is almost impossible to fail.

Network Marketing is my true love. It's the greatest self-development course on the planet. It leaves you open to learn more about yourself and others than almost anything else you can do.

Network Marketing is one of the few professions where you can watch and be part of turning wallflowers into rose gardens.

Bill Hyman had been in Network Marketing full time since 1979, growing a hugely successful organization of distributors in more than 100 countries. He is the co-author of Chicken Soup for the Network Marketer's Soul *along with Jack Canfield and Mark Victor Hansen. See www.MLMSoul.com*

How to Ruin Rapport

This chapter provided ways to put people at ease so they will be open to engaging with you again and again. Successful relationships take time and care to cultivate. You don't toss a handful of seeds on the ground and expect them to yield a harvest tomorrow. Don't sabotage your efforts by committing any of the following four rapport-breakers:

1. Making negative comments about your competition will work against your efforts at building rapport. People who hear you bad mouth someone can easily imagine you talking against them.

2. Talking when you should be listening can undo any goodwill you've built. Sales-type people often run on at the mouth without regard for the prospect. If you are doing this, shut up more and pay attention to what the customer is saying.

3. Discussing controversial topics can destroy rapport forever. Never talk about religion or politics. You can suddenly find you are the enemy instead of the problem solver.

4. Taking sides when family members disagree will bomb. All you will do is make someone angry. When there's friction between people who live together, there may be reasons and a history of conflicts you cannot know about. If you find yourself in danger of being drawn into a storm of family disagreement, bow out graciously.

Checklist for this Chapter's Tactics

Place a check in the appropriate column for determining how or if you will use a tactic. Then return to your 7-sentence marketing plan - see Chapter 3 - and fill in the appropriate tactics in Step 4 of your plan.

Tactics In This Chapter	Using Well	Using, But Needs Work	Not Using	Not Right At This Time
12. Smiles and Greetings				
13. Body Language				
14. Active Listening				
15. Identifying Core Needs				
16. Linking Your Network to the World				
17. Using Stories				

"The universe is made of stories, not atoms."
~ Muriel Rukeyser ~

CHAPTER 7

PROMOTIONAL TOOLS: DON'T LEAVE HOME WITHOUT THEM

"The key to realizing a dream is to focus not on success but significance - and then even the small steps and little victories along your path will take on greater meaning."
~ Oprah Winfrey ~

Wherever you go, there are opportunities to leave a marketing message behind to work for you. This chapter teaches you how and where to use promotional tools to catch the attention of prospects and motivate them to get back with you.

Promotional tools help you leverage your availability. You can hand someone a CD or brochure instead of repeating the same pitch time and again.

Professionally prepared materials add credibility to your offer. A multimedia DVD with interviews from satisfied customers and certified practitioners can instill confidence. Guerrillas always have promotional tools with them wherever they go, because they know having something to hand someone on a moment's notice generates always-on marketing.

Almost all network marketing companies sell a variety of marketing materials for distributor use, sparing you the time and hassles of creating your own. A wide range of generic tools are also available from independent suppliers (see the Appendix for a list of providers.) If the tools we describe here are not available, create your own, making sure they meet with your company's approval.

For your part, include your website, phone number, address, and e-mail on every brochure, catalog, article reprint, and anything else you hand a prospect. Simplify the process by printing up return address labels or get a rubber stamp with your contact information.

Promotional tools described in this chapter include, but are not limited to the items following. Consider creating a checklist of these materials so you'll know when you are running low and can replenish your supply.

- Sound bites
- Testimonials
- Business cards
- Brochures
- Catalogs
- Article reprints
- Tip sheets
- Research studies
- CDs and DVDs
- Bookmarks
- Toll-free number
- Voice mail
- Recorded info by phone
- Bumper stickers and Buttons
- Product samples

Be careful not to overload a prospect with information. Having a wide range of promo materials may suggest sending one of everything to a prospect. However, the recipient may easily feel overwhelmed and simply trash most of the materials. Before sending someone anything, ask permission first; you may be surprised to learn the person only chooses to have a catalog in order to place an order.

TACTIC 18. SOUND BITES

A sound bite or slogan consists of a few words which help set your product or opportunity apart. It is your unique strategic positioning in a short, memorable phrase, like "Finger-lickin' good" for KFC or "Just do it" for Nike. The title of this chapter was based on the sound bite, "Don't leave home without it," popularized by American Express. If your company doesn't already use a sound bite, create one.

Your sound bite should:

• Describe your product or service's benefit

• Express why your offer is better than your competition's

• Tell the customer why she should buy from you

Sound bites are examples of memes, a word originated by scientist Richard Dawkins, which refers to a unit of cultural information transferable from one human to another. Memes are distinct memorable units; they often spur viral marketing; and they convey a clear benefit.

To be useful, a sound bite should make your message memorable. A well-composed sound bite is brief, catchy, and to the point.

Your 7-Word Marketing Message

Your sound bite can be a 7-word message that you can say to anyone you meet on a moment's notice. Why seven words? A short phrase is easy for you and your prospects to remember.

Choose carefully, because your words must set you, your product, or your opportunity apart from the hundreds of competing marketing messages the average person is bombarded with daily.

Your 7-word message will have more impact when it boasts a strong benefit that entices people to say, "oh that's interesting, how do you do that." Hook their attention enough to open the door to setting an appointment or a follow up call.

A sound bite we use for this book is "100 ways to grow your warm list." We chose a strong benefit anyone in network marketing can relate to and we quantified it with a number to give it more impact. An example of a sound bite for skin care products could go something like, "fresh, radiant looking skin without dangerous chemicals."

MLM companies often sell promotional shirts, jackets, calendars, notepads, balloons, and all kinds of nifty little items to help you brand yourself like: personalized refrigerator magnets, Post-It® note pads, pens, caps, mugs, and other freebies. When your budget allows, find promotional items you can customize with your 7-word sound bite.

When opportunity shows itself, you can stand out with less than seven words like Fiona Cosham does.

Being Memorable
by Fiona Cosham

When I started selling Tupperware in Georgia with a British accent and an uncommon name, I wondered how I would be accepted. My name is Fiona, and every time I introduced myself, I had to say my name several times before people deciphered it, and then the response was usually "You mean like Princess Fiona in *Shrek*?"

Eventually I stopped being offended and decided to embrace the joke. I now introduce myself to customers as "Princess Fiona" and have named my team "Princess Plastics."

Luckily, far from alienating me, my accent is treated as a novelty factor, and at parties I often hear "I've only come to listen to you speak" or "I could listen to you talk all night." And yes, they do buy.

The point is simply this: if there is something about you that you think makes you different (even if no one else notices it), use it to your advantage. Turn a disability/disadvantage into an ability/advantage.

I am not making light of people with disabilities. I worked for a time with the disabled at the unemployment office. One of my favorite clients had a prosthetic hand he used to give to me, asking, "Do you need a hand?" I still remember him.

Remember: In sales, a novelty factor is what makes you stand out from your competition and what makes people remember you.

See Princess Fiona of Tupperware at
www.my.tupperware.com/princessfiona.

TACTIC 19. TESTIMONIALS

Confidence is often cited as the number one reason people buy anything. Third-party endorsements foster a sense of trust. Testimonials instill buyer confidence through providing social proof; if enough other people say a product works, it must be so.

When you say something about yourself or your offer, your listener thinks it may or may not be true, because they know you are self-motivated. If someone else—especially an authority—talks about you or your product, it's taken as evidence.

Testimonials cost you nothing to acquire. Your company already includes customer comments on its marketing materials and website. Create a folder or file to collect and list customer and distributor endorsements so you can pick and choose the best ones to include on your own hand-outs.

Testimonials are usually written in the customer's own words, are surrounded by quotation marks, and are attributed to the individual. They can be used in sales letters, brochures and advertisements.

Guerrilla	My network marketing
Affirmation	activities produce
	progressive results from using
	an *assortment* of tactics. I
	make use of the synergy of
	multiple marketing methods.

Endorsements get more response when they state a benefit measured in specific results. For instance, "I lost 37 pounds in 30 days" is more persuasive than "This weight loss product is great."

Quotes from such professionals as doctors, Ph.D.s, and practitioners validate product claims and instill customer confidence. Testimonials from research studies at major universities also endow credibility. According to Robert Cialdini, Ph.D. and author of the best-selling book, *Influence*, when experts are quoted, readers have a subconscious sense of obligation to believe an authority's statements. Did you notice how we just quoted an expert to authenticate a point?

More quotes that persuade are comments excerpted from magazine, newspaper, radio or TV shows. The cost to quote the media is zero; when comments come from television, magazines, or from published studies, you may freely quote the source publicly.

The more popular the media, the more social proof will urge compliance. Have you ever noticed how major brand name companies run commercials where they show one consumer after another testifying as to why they use the product?

Satisfied customers make excellent endorsers. They may even volunteer comments without any prompting from you or you can ask them to write a few words about their product results. When collecting testimonials from customers, ask for written permission to use the person's words along with their full name, credential if any, and city and state. Citing a person's full name and location builds credibility. Get even more persuasive power by inserting a photo of the person giving the testimonial.

Make a one-page hand-out listing your most compelling quotes. Send it to prospects as a follow-up. Pull from your list of testimonials when composing ads or other marketing pieces. For greater impact on your website, include audio clip testimonials from experts and satisfied users.

Tactic 20. Business Cards

Exchanging business cards is the most common form of introduction with someone you've just met. They cost little to print, yet provide a convenient way for people to remember each other. Business cards serve to remind people how to reach you, so include several means of contact, including: name, company, address, phone, e-mail, website, instant messenger, and fax.

The blank space on the back of business cards provides added opportunities like:

• Grab attention with a unique selling proposition, like   "Helping Eliminate Joint Pain Forever."

• Print an endorsement from a satisfied customer.

• Use the reverse side of your business card as a coupon. For example, print "Present this card for a free dinner next Thursday evening at _____" as an offer for a free meal in return for listening to a presentation of your opportunity.

• When talking to a prospect who has handed you his card, use the back to take notes about the person—likes, dislikes, family information.

• If you have distributors in other countries, print your information in other languages on the back of your card.

MLM companies often list designated printer-partners in brochures and on websites, from whom you can select a template business card. Using a personal computer and printer, you can also create your own business card using alternative size, material, color, fonts, images, and text. You can probably get a high-resolution image of the company logo to include on your cards. When printing from home, only use the best card stock with clean, crisp edges to give a professional look.

Here's some points to consider to make your business cards memorable:

• A clean looking, professionally printed and attractive card projects a great first impression.
• Choose a type font and size that is easy to read.
• Use 2 colors of ink or more.
• Include a catchy phrase like, "I'm making money while relaxing on cruises, are you?"
• Proofread your copy for errors before printing.
• Include your photo on your cards.
• Always have cards with you whenever you leave the house.
• Keep a good supply of cards, order ahead so you don't run out.
• Make a business card magnet; it will last longer than paper and can easily be placed on metal objects, filing cabinets, and refrigerators at home.
• Consider a 4-page or 8-page mini-brochure that folds into the size of a business card.

Cards are an inexpensive way to market. Give them out:

• Whenever you tip a taxi driver or waitress

- When paying bills
- To the bank clerk when making deposits
- When asking for referrals
- In line, while you're waiting anywhere.

TACTIC 21. BROCHURES

Brochures provide essential information about your company, product, or opportunity in an easy-to-read format. Brochures save you time by answering common questions and concerns. They are a great way to break the ice with someone you've just met. They can also act as a small step in warming a prospect up on the way to getting him to take another step, like a meeting.

Effective brochures provide images of happy people, bulleted lists of benefits, and raving testimonials from satisfied customers. They can be used as introductions or as follow-ups. Most MLM companies sell product and opportunity brochures in bulk. All you have to do is add your contact information.

"Opportunities multiply as they are seized."
~ Sun Tzu ~

TACTIC 22. CATALOGS

Marketing with your product catalog allows you to present the company's full range of products and services with visual impact to consumers. Statistics show people love shopping through mail order catalogs—catalog sales hit $68 billion in 2000.

Mail catalogs to previous customers. According to one survey 36 percent of people shop by mail because of the convenience and ease.

Leave catalogs at laundromats and in waiting rooms in hospitals and practitioner's offices. Have your contact information and distributor number generously placed throughout each catalog. That way, when a shopper places an order from a catalog, she can give your ID to the company.

Product catalogs will cost you more per copy than most of your other marketing pieces, but they provide your customers a wide selection of items from which to choose. Super stores like Home Depot and WalMart may have little else in common with network marketing, but they have proven the formula that success comes from offering their customers a broad range of products.

For customers who express interest in only one of your products, send a product sheet instead of a catalog. Many MLMs provide a library of individual product sheets you can download from their website and print at home or e-mail to prospects. Remember to include your personal contact information.

TACTIC 23. ARTICLE REPRINTS

Article reprints about your product or industry make great marketing pieces, even when they don't mention your company by name. For instance, if online travel is your service, feature articles written in major publications like *The Wall Street Journal* about the rise in online booking will help provide evidence of market demand to prospective distributors.

Promoting nutrition or enhanced athletic performance? The major magazines are loaded with articles on health and fitness. Look for feature editorials which point out benefits your product offers. In general, you can freely extract brief quotes from magazines and other media without permission as long as you give proper credit to the article's author and media source.

Turn your computer into a 24-hour a day article scout. Go to www.news.google.com and look for the link to "News Alerts." Google will e-mail you whenever a news article containing keywords related to your topic shows up online. For instance, if you are promoting a legal service and working the angle of credit collections for small business owners, you can have Google e-mail you notice of new articles with the phrase "bad debt." You'll soon have an arsenal of authoritative material from which to quote or to show reprints of to prospects.

Tactic 24. Tip Sheets

The more ways a product or service can be used, the higher its perceived value will be. Create a one-page tip sheet for each of your popular products on how to get the most from them. Tip sheets help customers with product ideas for getting tasks done easier.

Include ways to use your item that helps save money, saves time, or enhances health or beauty. If your items are consumable, come up with a recipe tip sheet.

Your parent company may already have a collection of usage tips you can use. Collect these and tips from your own customers.

At the bottom of each of your tip sheets, include your contact information and how to order.

Tactic 25. Research Studies

Like articles from well-known media, studies from universities or organizations instill trust in the reader. Your company doesn't have to be mentioned in a study in order for you to hitch a ride on the credibility wagon. For example, if you were selling a product with colostrum, there are plenty of university studies showing generic colostrum's beneficial effects with various health challenges. Universities conduct studies on a wide range of topics from memory loss, to social behavior, to health and nutrition.

Another plus of using excerpts from research studies is that universities are considered halls of authority. People are naturally swayed by credentials; most university studies are conducted by M.D.s and Ph.D.s.

Tactic 26. CDs and DVDs

As marketing tools, CDs and DVDs have the power to stimulate and engage listeners and viewers with greater impact than printed materials. They are inexpensive to reproduce and the cost of mailing disks is very low because of their light weight.

Students learn more and retain more when video is used in teaching, according to studies by the National Teaching Training Institute. Viewers stay more engaged. Eighty-five percent of teachers find that students are more engaged when television is used when teaching. Ninety percent of teachers report that their students learn more; eighty-nine percent say students retain more with instructional video.

Tactic 27. Bookmarks

Make bookmarks with usage tips for your best-selling products. Bookmarks are easy to create on a home computer and printer using card stock paper.

For example, your supplement alleviates arthritis pain. Create a bookmark that highlights how your product makes a difference. Include a testimonial on your bookmarks and tell how readers can reach you for more information.

Take the bookmarks to your public library, look up the popular book titles on arthritis, and place your bookmark within the books.

TACTIC 28. TOLL-FREE NUMBER

Toll-free numbers have been proven to boost response rates. Promote your company's toll-free order number to your distributors. They cost customers nothing to dial in to place orders.

It costs you nothing to promote your company-provided, toll-free order line. If you don't have the order number memorized, have it printed on your business cards and brochures.

Caution: only promote the company's toll-free number to those you've already signed up or to prospects who will have your ID number when calling in. Otherwise, you may lose prospects who simply sign up directly under the company.

If you place paid advertising, it may pay you to get your own toll-free number. According to AT&T, people are seven times more likely to call a toll-free number than a number they have to pay for.

Not having to pay for the call makes it easy for someone reading your ad to pick up the phone and dial. Most responders to ads are acting impulsively. The toll-free call eliminates any barrier which might delay the impulse to call, which could disappear in a short time.

Adding your own toll-free number is easy. Charges for incoming calls can be less than $.03 per minute. You can set it up so that calls to your toll-free number are routed to your land-line; you don't have to pay for a

Guerrilla Affirmation

I am *assertive* rather than aggressive in promoting my network marketing product and opportunity and supporting my team.

separate line. Compare toll-free providers at www.gmmlm.com/tollfree/.

"Many attempts to communicate are nullified by saying too much."
~ Robert Greenleaf ~

TACTIC 29. VOICE MAIL

When you're gone from home, your voice mail is still there communicating your message to incoming callers. Your message should be upbeat and tell callers they can expect a quick return call.

Update your recorded message monthly to include your company's newest product or bonus program. People will call just to get the news.

Do your callers a big favor; get an answering machine or voice mail provider that gives you the capacity to record messages that are longer than 60 seconds. It should be able to record a message for at least five minutes. Don't risk annoying callers who get cut off when leaving a message.

Some people won't leave a message no matter how positive you sound. Get Caller-ID service and you will be able to call back those who just dialed your phone and hung up instead of leaving a message.

When you are making calls and getting voice mail, here are several tips:

• Speak up so the person can hear you.

• Be enthused, positive, and at ease. Leave your message as you would talk to the person like you've known them for years.

• Mention a benefit which your prospect will gain from calling you back, like a way to save money on the person's first order.

• When leaving your phone number, say the numbers slowly once and then repeat the number again.

• When you call back a second or third time, change your message to include something new that you did not mention before.

• When calling leads who don't know you, mention that you are calling them back to follow up on their response to an opportunity ad.

• Practice leaving voice mail messages to yourself. Go over what you are going to say beforehand so your voice can come across with confidence.

• Be prepared to leave a brief message when you reach answering machines with short tapes.

TACTIC 30. RECORDED INFO BY PHONE

Many MLM companies offer a recorded product or opportunity message to refer prospects to. Referring people to recorded information by phone is practical when you're sponsoring long distance and you aren't sure what time zone someone will be calling from.

MLM companies play prerecorded marketing messages whenever a caller is placed on hold. Exploit this underused marketing tool by encouraging customers and distributors to take every opportunity to call the company. They'll get the latest news and updates and it won't cost you or them a penny because you've dialed in on the company's toll-free line.

An effective tactic is to prequalify leads by sending them to a prerecorded marketing message for your opportunity like the one described in the following story.

One Appointment for Every Three Dials
Beatty Carmichael

Having been in this industry for years, I have learned that calling leads is mostly a numbers game. Typically you only connect with one out of every three to four leads you buy. You get voice-mail, disconnected numbers and sometimes just plain "no answers."

Setting appointments is when the fun begins. You know what I mean if you've been calling leads for any length of time. You have to talk with all kinds of people before finding those really interested in looking.

A friend of mine generates her own, online leads using a one-page "teaser" site that got people to call her Sizzle Line®. So I decided to test this method with leads I bought.

I used "real time *redirect* leads" from www.successleadsonline.com. These are leads that, as soon as people fill out their web forms to become a lead, they are *immediately* redirected to any website you choose.

So, I bought these leads and had them redirected to my Sizzle Line® website. I felt those who called were probably the most interested... and I was right.

It was almost a week before I got around to calling my leads. When I dialed those who called my Sizzle Line, *every one* of the numbers were good. On my FIRST try, I called nine people. 4 weren't home. Of the other 5, I set 3 appointments. That's one appointment for every 3 dials I made ... unbelievable!

When I tried the other leads who didn't call the Sizzle Line®. I got disconnected numbers, uninterested people and more. Sure, there were a few interested ones, but I had to wade through a lot more leads to find them.

This story was contributed by GrowthPro, which helps network marketers find their own leads or filter the leads they buy. For more information, visit www.GrowthPro.com/book/

TACTIC 31. BUMPER STICKERS AND BUTTONS

Bumper stickers and buttons advertise your offer while you are going about your normal activities. They both offer cheap ways to get your message seen every day.

Have you ever not read a bumper sticker on the back of the car in front of you? Even corny ones get noticed. Bumper stickers continue working for you even when your car is just sitting in a parking space.

Bumper stickers or buttons don't require a lot of text. In fact, the shorter, the better. They make great venues for your 7-word sound bite or unique selling proposal. Just tag on your web address or phone number and your car or button becomes a roaming mini-billboard. You can also apply stickers to large envelopes or packages when sending mail.

Check your company's catalog for promotional aids or create your own stickers at www.makestickers.com.

TACTIC 32. SAMPLES

Giving out free samples lets people quickly learn if your product or service is for them. If your product is as good as your sales aids say it is, a majority of the people who try the sample will order.

When looking at your costs for giving out free samples, remember that most other forms of advertising require the costs of repetition, whereas sampling is a one-time expense. When you offer a free sample and the customer is happy about their experience, you've won them over in a friendly, personable way, something advertising can't do. Free samples let you initiate instant rapport and build a bridge for further communication.

More things to remember about using free samples as a marketing tactic:

Guerrilla Affirmation

When making calls to customers, I will never hang up the phone before them. I will wait for them to hang up first, so I never give the impression that I can't wait to get on to the next call.

- Only give out samples when the quality of the product is so good, people feel an immediate result.
- Whenever possible, include your contact information on the packaging.
- Require a person's contact information in exchange for the free sample, so you can follow up.
- If your budget is tight, don't advertise a free sample offer; you will attract freebie hunters that will quickly exhaust your supply. Provide free samples one person at a time as you are talking to people. It will make each person feel special.
- If you offer a service rather than a product, let prospects "test-drive" your service free for a limited time.

Where to Leave Promotional Material

Get the most return on your investment in marketing materials by being choosey where you leave them. Place materials in reach of your target audiences where they hang out, where they work, and where they wait for services.

For instance, if you're promoting a nutritional product, your articles, fact sheets, or newsletters have a good chance of getting picked up and read in waiting rooms for doctors, chiropractors, and hospitals.

Here's a list of locations which attract crowds who may read your materials:

• Apartment leasing offices
• Bank and credit union waiting areas
• Bookstore entrances with other free publications
• Bowling alleys
• Dressing rooms
• Fitness centers
• Employee lunch rooms
• Hair and nail salons
• Health food and grocery store announcement boards
• Include in envelope when you pay your bills
• Laundry mats and dry cleaners
• Practitioner's waiting rooms: acupuncturist, chiropractor, doctor, dentist, orthodontist, veterinarian, hospital, medical clinic
• Professional services waiting rooms: accountant, attorney, insurance, real estate, mortgage, employment agency
• Public libraries
• Recreation and senior activity centers
• Restaurants, coffee stops, ice cream shops
• Supply stores announcement boards
• Tanning salons
• Teacher lounges
• Yoga or dance studios
• Public waiting areas (movies, airports, bus terminals, taxi stands, check-out lines, etc.)

Wearing promotional items like t-shirts can spark conversations which lead to building relationships, as Randy Gage reports.

Overcoming Shyness
By Randy Gage

I came into the business as a pathologically shy person, with very poor social skills. We could talk about my childhood and why that was, but what's the point? It was what it was.

However, even as a shy person, I put myself in positions where I was able to meet lots of people, and do it in a way that wasn't so threatening for me. All I was really doing was living life. And while I did that, I met a bunch of people. Let me give you some examples.

I have been a baseball fan my whole life. But I was a nerdy bookworm growing up, and never played sports. My mother didn't have money for leagues and equipment, so I never played Little League, and since I was expelled from school at sixteen, you know I certainly didn't play in high school or college.

Then, at the age of forty, I played in a charity softball tournament and had the time of my life. I realized I could now play whenever I wanted to. So I went back home and found an ad for a softball league and I joined.

The day of the first game, I was deathly nervous because I was going to meet ten or twelve guys I had never met. But my love of softball overcame my fear and I went. Of course, as soon as we started playing, I forgot all about fear and had a wonderful time. I had a dozen new friends. Then I started meeting guys on other teams. Today I have a Manager, a Director, and a Double Diamond Director in my business–because I met them in the softball league.

I wanted to develop my speaking skills, so I joined a speakers association. Sure, I was nervous going to the first meeting. But the people there all shared the same interests I did, and I soon relaxed. Today I have a Manager, Director, and Senior Director in my business–because I met them in that organization. I have a Regional Director because I go to a certain church, and another because of a seminar I attended.

Even as a shy person, I put myself in situations where I was forced to meet people. But I met them in an area of shared interest, or common experiences. And anyone, you included, can do this. It is a question of putting yourself in "relate-ability" situations and the appropriate networks.

By relate-ability, I mean putting yourself in situations where people around you can relate to you. I call this the "Georgia Tech factor" because of a situation I often experience. Let me explain. I was playing in a softball tournament in Atlanta, and it poured rain the whole weekend. My uniform was soaked, so I stopped in a campus bookstore and bought some running shorts, t-shirt and cap, which naturally had the Georgia Tech logo on them. So now and then I pull one of these items out of the drawer to wear when I go out to do my morning cardio.

Invariably someone will exclaim, "Oh you went to Georgia Tech, too?" The same thing happens when I wear the Boston College t-shirt I bought under similar circumstances. People who went to these schools instantly relate to me (and start conversations) because they believe we have a shared experience.

Even a shy person can put himself or herself in a position where others will relate to them —and even start conversations with them on a daily basis. If you are in line with 800 people to see the new *Star Wars* movie or to buy the latest Harry Potter book, that is a shared experience, and provides a chance to make new friends.

Any time you're sharing an experience with others, you have the opportunity to meet people and develop relationships. That doesn't mean you should try and sponsor them on the street corner. I'm just saying you should go out and live life. And while doing that, you will meet people. And if you nurture those relationships, many of those people could be good candidates for your business. And even if they're not, you'll make some great friends.

For me, the results have been amazing. I took the business quite seriously, and I have given more than 600 people the opportunity to look at what I have. Of those, I personally sponsored 97 of them. About half of them disappeared from the radar screen within a month or two of joining. Some still use the products; many don't even do that.

The 40-something distributors that stayed around have now duplicated into a group of over 35,000. Of course they all aren't active; some are just customers, while others are serious about building a business. But that group produced sales for my company of over $2.5 million last month. So that has created a residual income for me of over one million dollars a year. Not bad for a shy high school dropout!

Randy Gage is the author of seven books, including, How to Build a Multi-Level Money Machine. *You can learn more about him at www.randygage.com.*

Over time, your promotional toolbox will grow. However, be conservative when encouraging your new team members to purchase tools. You may find yourself with unhappy new distributors who blame you for getting them to put out money for promotional material instead of helping them earn a check.

Keep your costs down by purchasing in quantities that get you a discount. Contact members in your organization and other legs of other distributors for putting together a big order that saves everyone money.

Whatever you do, don't run out of anything. Avoid giving the appearance of being unprofessional with excuses like, "I'm sorry, I'm out of cards today." Have materials with you wherever you go, whether it's a supply of business cards, CDs, or catalogs.

Guerrilla Affirmation

I *consistently* take action steps based on my marketing plan and evaluate my plan regularly to improve how it works for me.

Checklist for this Chapter's Tactics

Place a check in the appropriate column for determining how or if you will use a tactic. Then return to your 7-sentence marketing plan - see Chapter 3 - and fill in the appropriate tactics in Step 4 of your plan.

Tactics In This Chapter	Using Well	Using, But Needs Work	Not Using	Not Right At This Time
18. Sound Bites				
19. Testimonials				
20. Business Cards				
21. Brochures				
22. Catalogs				
23. Article Reprints				
24. Tip Sheets				
25. Research Studies				
26. CDs and DVDs				
27. Bookmarks				
28. Toll-Free Number				
29. Voice Mail				
30. Recorded Info by Phone				
31. Bumper Stickers and Buttons				
32. Samples				

CHAPTER 8

THE MONEY IS
IN YOUR LIST

---

*"The meeting of two personalities is like the
contact of two chemical substances: if there
is any reaction, both are transformed."*
~ Carl Jung ~

Imagine this scenario: you've built a large network marketing organization with a new company that just launched a year ago. The company suddenly announces it is filing bankruptcy. Distributors won't receive their checks and no more orders are going out to customers. Sounds pretty grim, but this kind of situation has happened to many people.

The guerrilla network marketer knows that the real money isn't in a particular opportunity or product; it's in the people. Guerrillas build their lists from a loyal following, because that's where the money is. Should circumstances force you to change companies, the people in your organization won't follow you just because you were in their upline. But they will follow you if you've treated them with warmth, integrity, and respect.

Using guerrilla tactics, you can accumulate hundreds of new prospects every month at a minimum investment. Remember though, gathering leads will amount to little, unless you have a system to transform those names on your list into relationships.

Your marketing activities should create a funnel that gathers leads, establishes rapport, and gets appointments. That's all. You don't try to persuade, convince, or sell anything until you can get your prospect's agreement to meet—either by phone or in person.

Once your prospect agrees to an appointment, you have both taken the first step to creating a business relationship.

This chapter will help you grow your list through:
• Using a contact management system
• Adding names through referrals
• Buying leads
• Renting mailing lists
• Prospecting leads online
• Meeting your neighbors

Tactic 33. Using a Contact Management System

Before you begin gathering leads, set up a contact management system that will help you enter, store, and manage every contact's information.

Being able to access contact information easily eliminates the stress of forgetting where you recorded notes about someone.

Record notes from conversations—family and work details—that will allow you to pick up a conversation using talking points gathered previously. People love it when you remember what's going on in their lives. It shows you care.

Your contact management system should be capable of generating address labels to send out mailings, e-mail addresses to send announcements, and phone numbers to call. It should be searchable and sortable by name, city, distributor rank, status of lead or prospect, etc.

To do this job, many businesses use *Microsoft Access* or *Excel. ACT!* is also considered to be an excellent contact manager. Whatever system you use, become so familiar with its workings that you can instantly access the information, however you choose to sort it.

Most word processing programs include a function called "mail merge." Mail merge allows you to create a personalized letter to different people by automatically inserting the person's name and other information any place in the document. The more personalized your letters are, the greater the response you can expect.

A contact management system lets you send out e-mail announcements to a specific group. You can create different groups according to level of involvement. For example, you might create a group with contact information of only new customers, another group of distributors, and still another group of leaders.

Some of the more technical-savvy services that sell leads provide a built-in contact manager. The system sends a series of pre-programmed autoresponder e-mails designed to get the person to contact you.

Whichever system you adopt, start by adding in the names and information from your warm list—which is your first asset in your network marketing business. Protect this valuable asset by backing up the data file regularly to a CD or DVD, in case of a computer failure.

Tactic 34. Adding Names Through Referrals

Network marketing companies have always relied on the far-reaching effects of word-of-mouth referrals from satisfied customers. Life-changing products can easily generate multiple generations of referrals just by people telling their friends about their experiences.

Some new distributors imagine they know only a small number of people and therefore may see a small potential audience. Once you show them that the potential for prospects is not just who they know, but who their contacts know—and who those people know—that the power of network marketing begins to dawn.

Guerrilla
Affirmation

I measure my success by how many new *relationships* I've made each month, because people prefer to do business with people they like.

When a person gives you a referral, you've gained the advantage of being able to mention the first person in your conversation with the referral, immediately positioning yourself as a friend of a friend or associate.

If a referral has an experience with the product or earns a fast-track bonus, you can go back to the original referrer and make a case for him to join.

To spark word-of-mouth referrals, your service or product has to create an immediate result from which the user benefits—the quicker, the better. The response you are seeking is, "Wow, this really works!"

There's a right time to ask for referrals. The optimum time to make your request is when a customer is at a high level of satisfaction. This is when he or she is most likely to give you another person's name. It costs you nothing to ask, so take that one extra step to get additional business from every customer. Make asking for referrals a habit.

TACTIC 35. BUYING LEADS

There are many services that provide leads for sale to network marketers. Typically, these are names and contact information of people who have responded to a home-business opportunity ad.

Some providers offer real-time leads, which means the person has just filled in a request for more information and you are e-mailed their name and contact information at once. Since the person is thinking about finding a business at that moment, get back with him or her right away. The longer you delay, the more distant the opportunity seeker's impulse to take further action becomes.

An advantage of buying leads is that you know the people are actively looking for a suitable business. A disadvantage is that, in many cases, opportunity lead lists are sold over and over again. Many of the people may have already been prospected by other network marketers. If this is the case, consider changing to a leads provider who doesn't resell leads multiple times.

When shopping for leads, ask the following questions of the provider:

- How old are the leads?
- How many other buyers will get the same leads?
- Will you receive phone, e-mail, and postal address?
- Has the lead filled in a questionnaire that qualifies the person as a business opportunity seeker?
- Did the person receive an incentive to submit a form such as getting paid to take a survey?

Ask your upline if they've purchased leads and what the results were. If you are considering working with a specific leads provider, see if you can find someone who has used their leads with success. See the list of providers in the resource appendix and at www.gmmlm.com/leads.htm.

Regardless of how you gather leads, you still have to qualify who you'll work with. Tim Sales has a simple but effective tactic for identifying potential builders.

Why You Need To Dream
by Tim Sales

While some conditions in network marketing have changed over the years, one main one has not. And perhaps it's this one thing that people are really asking for. This thing hasn't changed in the fifteen years I've been in MLM, nor is it likely to change in the next century.

The thing I'm talking about is the answer to the question, "Will I?" versus "Can I?" Put another way, "Will I do it?" versus "Can I do it?"

When I first joined MLM, I most certainly could not do it. But I was willing to learn to do those things that I evidently couldn't do based on my results. I came to set this as a basic requirement for who I sponsor and work with, versus who I don't sponsor and work with.

The difference between success and failure is one's ability to see and recognize the difference between "Can I?" and "Will I?" If one only asks, "Can I do it?" then the answer is normally "No." That leads to either not starting at all or quitting.

I first realized this difference as a boy of ten years old. I read the first book of my life—*Where the Red Fern Grows*, by Wilson Rawls. It was and still is the greatest inspirational book I've ever read. The story is about a boy who lives in the country and really wants two coon-hunting dogs. The personal development part is about what he goes through to earn enough money to buy his dogs, and then later how and what he does to train his dogs to hunt.

The boy in the story and I had a lot in common. I, too, lived in the country and was fascinated by raccoons. Also, like the boy in the story, my family didn't have a lot of money. I didn't use the book to figure out how to get two coon-hunting dogs; I used it to get a bicycle. But it wasn't just *any* bike—it was a top-of-the-line ten-speed with disc brakes.

I sold worms to the local fishing store for $1.50. I picked blackberries for $3 a bucket. I mowed yards for $5, raked leaves for $7 and cleaned up construction sites for

$10. I did this for two years to get enough money for the bike. The day I brought that bike home and rode down the street with the wind on my face and tears in my eyes was the day I realized that my dreams do come true and that victory is worth the effort.

What I learned from the book and my success in getting the bike had much to do with success I later achieved in wrestling, in the military, and in network marketing. Without that inspiration, I don't know if I would have even joined network marketing, or ever come up with the training that has helped so many.

That event set in motion a "success formula" for me.

1. I realized that I was again in a situation where it was evident that I didn't know how to do it—but, as before I wouldn't let that stop me.

2. I realized that EVERYTHING looks confusing and impossible in the beginning. The trick is to take a big chunk of stuff that's confusing and cut it in half; once I understand the first half, I pick up the other half and figure that out.

3. I realized that I had to keep my eye on the goal, not on the little problems, like people saying no and people quitting. When focused on getting my first bike, I dug up worms for four hours and walked to the store, only to have the owner tell me he would only buy the night crawlers (a specific type of worm.) There were hundreds of people that didn't want me to mow their yard. When I went to buy the bike, Sears had raised the price; that alone set me back two months.

Remember, it isn't JUST about specific actions. You must first be able to dream. And then you have to be able to be inspired.

The most difficult situation I face when training another person in MLM is when that person cannot get inspired. A person stops dreaming and stops getting inspired because he doesn't believe in himself to do what he says he will do. This person has to start back on simple things that are not very challenging, and prove to himself that he can and will do what he says he will do.

Imagine the person who says (to himself) that he will do these simple tasks, then doesn't. Each item is insignificant at face value. However, it's perhaps the most damaging thing in the world because now the person doesn't believe in himself. That is how a person ceases to dream, thus ceases to live.

Dream it, create it, enjoy it!

Tim Sales helps network marketers gain the confidence and skills to be successful. His training is based on his own achievement of building and leading an organization of 56,000 people around the globe. See www.brilliantexchange.com/blog.

TACTIC 36. RENTING MAILING LISTS

Another way to add names to your list is through renting targeted mailing lists to which you send out an offer. By acquiring lists of people who have demonstrated an interest in a topic, you can get your offer in front of niche audiences who are most likely to try your product.

You can rent lists of buyers of books on longevity or fitness, purchasers of specific products from mail-order catalogs, or subscribers to newsletters and magazines that relate to your field. You can rent lists of members of associations. There are lists of names to rent for almost any topic you can think of.

The cost of renting a list can run anywhere from $.05 per name to $.25 per name with the average list priced around $.10 to $.12 each. Usually, there is a minimum number you can rent, like 5,000 names. You may have the option to pay for a one-time use or, for a higher price, unlimited use.

When renting mailing lists, remember to learn:
• When was the list last updated?
• Are these people likely candidates for your offer?
• Is there some compensation for bad addresses?

Unlike opportunity-seeker leads, most of your mailing list names will not be expecting your offer. Response rates vary enormously due to your offer, the timing, and the list. If you get a 2 percent or better response, you're doing well. But, you can't know what your response rate will be until you test. After your test, compare all your costs and sales and determine if the acquisition of new customers or distributors is worth the effort and expense to continue.

Remember, a new customer might buy several hundred dollars in products over the coming years, so renting lists may be worth the higher cost of acquisition in the long run.

You can rent lists directly from a publication or mail-order catalog. Or, you can go through a mail-list broker, who typically offers an online catalog of hundreds of lists to choose from. Check out the list of brokers and other resources from the Direct Marketing Association's website at www.thedirectmarketingsearch.com.

TACTIC 37. PROSPECTING LEADS ONLINE

Whether you are looking for leads, potential joint venture marketing partners, fairs and expos, associations, or individuals, online search will speed the process.

Here are examples of using search engines for gathering leads:

- Job sites like hotjobs.yahoo.com, elance.com, guru.com and monster.com allow you to view resumes for professionals that match your niche audience.
- Find associations of all types searchable by categories, including health, business, computers, and many more at the Internet Public Library at www.ipl.org/div/aon/.
- Learn about Internet discussion groups formed around topics related to your product or service. (For more on using the Internet, see Chapter 13.)

TACTIC 38. MEETING YOUR NEIGHBORS

Take an afternoon and go around your neighborhood introducing yourself to people and businesses you haven't met yet. People who've just moved into your neighborhood will appreciate the welcome. Being neighbors gives you something in common and an excuse to say hello. Keep introductions friendly. Get to know the people who live and work in your community; you don't have to prospect them. You will learn if you have enough in common that you will choose to get together with them again.

Checklist for this Chapter's Tactics

Place a check in the appropriate column for determining how or if you will use a tactic. Then return to your 7-sentence marketing plan - see Chapter 3 - and fill in the appropriate tactics in Step 4 of your plan.				
Tactics In This Chapter	Using Well	Using, But Needs Work	Not Using	Not Right At This Time
33. Using a Contact Management System				
34. Adding Names Through Referrals				
35. Buying Leads				
36. Renting Mailing Lists				
37. Prospecting Leads Online				
38. Meet Your Neighbors				

One of the best ways to compile bigger lists is to partner with other businesses and professionals who serve the same audiences you wish to reach. The next chapter describes how you can profit from partnering through fusion marketing.

CHAPTER 9

FUSION MARKETING

---

*"Success is liking yourself, liking what
you do, and liking how you do it."*
~ Maya Angelou ~

You can speed the process of growing your list by partnering with others who are already building trust with a pool of loyal clients and customers.

Every established business and profession has a network of clients. Many of these businesses offer services and products to the same customers who fit your target audience.

Through fusion marketing—promoting to other people's customer lists for mutual advantage—Guerrilla networkers leverage their list-building hundreds or thousands of times over. The tactics in this chapter will help you learn about:

• Partnering with businesses and professionals
• Partnering with associations, clubs, and groups

TACTIC 39. PARTNERING WITH BUSINESSES AND PROFESSIONALS

When you partner with other businesses, your message gets credibility by being seen alongside a trusted merchant or professional. Fusion marketing arrangements usually cost less than promotions you finance on your own. More reasons to seek out business partners include:

- You save time by leveraging your efforts to reach other lists.
- You can test more audiences with special offers.
- If you produce a newsletter, you'll grow your subscriptions.
- You will learn more about prospective audiences in the process of working with fusion marketing partners.
- You will gain more happy customers, some of whom will become distributors.
- You can attract more fusion marketing partners, because your business partner may refer you to his associates.
- You gain free access to qualified lists of prospects. The list gives you further opportunities to communicate marketing messages for related products.

By their nature, business owners are usually open to joint ventures, provided they are approached in the right way. They are already in business and selling something, so their thoughts revolve around adding potential profit streams.

Choosing the Right Fusion Marketing Partners

Begin your search for marketing partners the same way you would create a list of prospects for your product. Go back to your 7-sentence marketing plan and your list of product benefits and note which audiences are most likely to gain. Now, ask yourself what kind of businesses and professionals already serve those audiences?

A gas mileage-enhancing product is a good match for car washes, auto mechanics, tire stores, and auto supply stores. Aromatherapy oils will complement products available at a beauty salon, spa, massage clinic, or health food store. A legal service will tie in with insurance, real estate, and all kinds of small businesses.

>
> *Guerrilla Affirmation*
>
> Before contacting prospects for fusion marketing deals, I am totally confident in the benefits of my products and compensation plan so that I can offer many ways to help my business partners.

Identifying potential partners is as easy as flipping through the Yellow Pages, or use the Internet to research prospective partners. Type in keywords related to your topic and then visit the websites. To find local businesses, include your city when searching online.

Newsletter and ezine directory sites can also be helpful for locating experts in fields complementing yours who may be open to your offer. Find close to 3,000 online newsletters on different topics at <u>www.ezine-dir.com</u>. Ezine and newsletter publishers are sometimes open to joint venture opportunities as long as a proposal shows genuine income potential and pertains to their readers' interests.

When reviewing prospective partners, look for reputable businesses and organizations. These are your best potential allies because they are most likely to have gained the confidence and trust of the people you desire to reach.

Making a Joint Marketing Proposal

Professionals and business owners are busy people. Before you approach them, define your offer. Be able to articulate the gains for your fusion marketing partner. For network marketers, this will usually take the form of signing up customers and distributors directly under the partner.

Yours is probably not the first or only joint venture offer a business owner will receive. Make sure you get him a product sample early on. A business owner will not endorse a product he isn't sold on himself.

The business with the customers is the one with the leverage, not the network marketer with the product, regardless of how strongly you feel about the benefits of your offer. Every business owner feels protective of his flock.

To make the proposal appealing, offer to do any labor involved, like mailing and answering calls. Your gain is getting the leverage of a whole new group of prospects through the partner's influence.

For example, you propose to mail to a busy salon owner's client list. The offer will include a product sample, free report, or DVD about an innovative natural hair care product, along with a note that includes the stylist's recommendation. The stylist supplies the list of names and you do the mailing. You take care of call-ins and sign up customers and distributors under your partner. This kind of arrangement allows you to help the salon owner develop an additional income stream while introducing you to a qualified new audience.

Learn as much as you can about a prospective business owner or organization manager before making an approach. If you send a written proposal, your offer must appear relevant enough to get attention, and brief enough (one page is sufficient) that it isn't discarded.

In all your communications, use the person's first name and include points about the person's business, showing you took the time to know what he or she is about.

Show respect by asking the decision maker in an e-mail or brief phone call what is their preferred way of receiving a proposal. There is no one way to approach everyone. Learn what your prospect likes, and you'll earn points for making the effort to please.

The first questions in your prospective partner's mind are "What's in it for me?" and "What's in it for my clients?" The benefits of your offer comprise your value proposition. It should explain quickly and obviously what the prospective partner has to gain from working with you.

Your partner's clients will gain from getting exceptional product benefits that solve their pain. Benefits to the partner will include residual income and bring able to offer complementary products to their existing services.

Provide your prospect with reasons to feel confident about working with you. Include some brief background information about your credentials and experience or testimonials from other business owners you've partnered with.

Think of ways your offer will help your prospect advance his business faster than he could through his existing activities.

---

*"The most important trip you may take
in life is meeting people halfway."*
~ Henry Boye ~

Your fusion marketing proposal should not merely speculate about income, but show exactly where the money will come from.

After you've achieved measurable results with one fusion marketing partner, include those results in proposals to other prospective partners. If a satisfied partner agrees, see if he will give you a testimonial. Prospective partners are more likely to commit if they know you have existing relationships with other established organizations or business owners.

Make your partner aware there is no risk for him or his clients by offering a complete, money-back guarantee. Since most MLMs provide a satisfaction guarantee, the "at risk" factor is the parent company's, not yours.

Spell-check your proposal and proofread it to correct any grammatical errors. If you're sloppy in your proposal, it will give the impression that you're sloppy in everything else you implement.

TACTIC 40. JOINING ASSOCIATIONS AND LODGES

Join fraternal lodges like Rotary, Lion's Club, Kiwanis, and country clubs to meet business-minded people. Find associations related to your product's industry to network with other members and to learn about newsletters appropriate for renting subscriber lists.

Typically, associations publish a member's directory that lists contact information. Sometimes this contact data is listed online at the association's website in the member's only area.

"I have found no greater satisfaction than achieving success through honest dealing and strict adherence to the view that, for you to gain, those you deal with should gain as well."
~ Alan Greenspan ~

Learn how you can participate on committees and projects. Become a problem solver. You'll earn respect and find people coming to you about potential joint ventures.

There are thousands of local lodges and associations for different interest groups; over a dozen associations in North America are related to alternative medicine and more than eight associations revolve around women's health issues. Another eight associations address exercise and fitness. Find a huge list of associations accessible by categories at www.ipl.org/div/aon/.

Fusion Marketing Examples

• Host a seminar with a practitioner or related business on a popular health or related topic your product provides a solution for.

• Partner with a local radio by providing the producer with a list of frequently asked questions or top ten tips about a specific health, wealth or relationship problem that your product alleviates. Send the questions along with a brief bio and they may interview you or mention your website as a resource.

• Create a contest with a prize related to your product. Send an announcement to the list members of your fusion marketing partners.

• Offer a free trial to software related to your product or service. To find free programs, go to www.download.com and search for your product-related keywords. Contact appropriate marketing partners to offer the software to their lists. When prospects download or receive the software by mail, they also get your marketing message.

• Contact your community's home owner's association to learn if they provide welcome packages to new folks moving in. See if you can add a free product sample and your business card or brochure. If your neighborhood doesn't offer a welcome package, consider starting one.

• Check your Yellow Pages and community newspapers for ads for daycare centers. Call to find out the owner's name and send a catalog, CD, or DVD. Ask if they would be interested in an extra income stream in return for hosting home parties for parents of their kids.

• Offer to insert a flyer for another business along with your mailings. Ask the business to include your flyers in their mailings.

• Create an ebook with tips on solving a specific problem related to the audience's interest. Partner with a business that already reaches that audience to distribute the ebook as a customer service. Make sure your ebook provides real value and includes a link to your website for more information.

• Place free take-one boxes at retail locations. Offer a free gift in return for dropping in a business card or filled-in contact form.

• Approach bingo halls and pool halls with an offer to donate a prize (one of your best selling products) for their games and contests. Supply entry forms with your marketing message or website address.

• See if local small business owners are willing to let you place a flyer on their store window near the front door. They may even allow you to set up a small counter display showcasing your hottest-selling products. Offer them a percentage of all sales and the opportunity to sign up new distributors under them.

• For bath and beauty products, partner with home remodelers and builders to put a product display in bathrooms in a model home.

Checklist for this Chapter's Tactics

Place a check in the appropriate column for determining how or if you will use a tactic. Then return to your 7-sentence marketing plan - see Chapter 3 - and fill in the appropriate tactics in Step 4 of your plan.				
Tactics In This Chapter	Using Well	Using, But Needs Work	Not Using	Not Right At This Time
39. Partnering with Businesses and Professionals				
40. Joining Associations and Lodges				

CHAPTER 10
TACTICS FOR MEETINGS

"To pull together is to avoid being pulled apart."
~ Bob Allisat ~

Organized meetings provide a way to leverage your time by presenting to groups of people, rather than to individuals one by one. Speaking to crowds will help you achieve your goals faster.

This chapter gives you tactics for working with groups of people through:
- Company conventions
- Opportunity meetings
- Home parties
- Lead group meetings
- Sizzle sessions

TACTIC 41. COMPANY CONVENTION

There is probably no better tool for leveraging your efforts from a single activity as your company's convention. The advantages of getting yourself and everyone in your organization to your company convention include:
- Meeting other distributors. Social proof is a persuasive influence. By getting new and prospective distributors to a convention attended by hundreds or thousands of active members, you are proving that your opportunity is worth being involved in, because all the other attendees agree that it is, or they would not be

there. All you have to do is get there and bring all your people. The event does the rest.

• Meet the folks who manage and, in some cases, started the company. MLM company founder(s) are typically charismatic entrepreneurs who have attracted an experienced management team to help distributors grow their business. The marketing benefit to you comes from tapping into the influence of their authority as presenters of the event.

• Receive acknowledgement for people in your organization who have demonstrated leadership and advancement in rank.

• Get exclusive offers and special savings only available at conventions.

• Be the first to learn about new products, contests, bonuses, and incentives.

• Expand your knowledge through training sessions on product usage and business development.

• Acquire the feeling of being connected to something bigger than you. This fulfills a basic human desire for belonging.

• Exploit the opportunity to travel to an exciting convention location and have fun.

TACTIC 42. OPPORTUNITY MEETINGS

Opportunity meetings have been one of the foundational building tools in network marketing. They are a venue for presenting a compelling call to action. Because of the presence of others, meetings invoke social proof, and can also generate contagious excitement and enthusiasm.

Successful opportunity meetings are planned and have a flow that makes sense to the attendees. They come to a close in a way that leaves people longing for more.

Just because someone doesn't show up at a meeting after you've invited him, don't write him off or you might miss enrolling your next super star, like Richard Brooke.

Persuasive Compensation
by Richard Brooke

I grew up on an isolated ranch in central California and did not develop many social skills. I did not do well in school, lacked confidence, was generally negative, and didn't like other people. After high school I ended up working at a chicken processing plant. In 1974, my job was to cut chickens into various parts as they flew past me on the automated line. I earned $3.05 an hour, plus overtime.

One day, a friend of mine called the plant and told me to come to a meeting to hear how to earn a lot of money. He was mostly unemployed, other than some summer cannery work, and did not have a lot of credibility with me about money, so I passed.

Weeks later I happened by his house. He was having a party celebrating his first commission check for $1,874 after three weeks of being involved in this new opportunity. It was twice as much as I made working all month cutting the chickens.

So I spent a little time looking and listening. What I saw I had never seen or heard of before. It seemed unbelievable.

What I finally came to understand was an income and wealth-building system invented in the early 1950s. The inventors of the multilevel concept really just invented a compensation plan for a direct sales business. But they changed some traditional rules to make the compensation plan really sing.

The plan they presented suggested that a person could earn up to $5,000 a month, part time. That was three times what I earned cutting chickens full time. I got involved, even quit my job and pursued this opportunity with a passion. Initially, I was a miserable failure. I had to sell everything I owned—my house, my furniture, and my car— just to stay in the game. Eventually I broke loose and starting making the system work. By the time I was 28 I had earned my first million. Thirty thousand people spread over the entire U.S. earned me income every month.

In 1986, I set out to build a different model for an MLM company—one the public could trust, admire and respect. I committed to building Oxyfresh in such a way that I could help restore the image of our industry so the average person could see the extraordinary wealth building opportunity a residual income provides.

Twenty-one years later, I am proud of what Oxyfresh has become. We are a respected network marketing industry leader that has helped thousands of people around the world create a life of financial freedom and personal independence.

Richard Bliss Brooke is President of Oxyfresh.com and founder of High Performance People, LLC. He is a sought-after personal development and leadership coach, speaker and author of Mach II: The Art of Personal Vision and Self Motivation; Mailbox Money: The Promise of Network Marketing *and* The Four Year Career™. *See* www.RichardBrooke.com.

Outline for an Opportunity Meeting

• Meet guests at the door as they enter.

• When beginning, make a brief introduction to edify the main speaker.

• Schedule ten to fifteen minutes of live testimonials.

• Play a company presentation DVD or present a company overview using visual aids.

• If possible, do a product demonstration where people can see immediate results.

• When possible, create a total experience by engaging the five senses through including visuals (with displays,) sound (from music,) touch (by greeting people with a handshake on arrival and departure,) and taste (by offering product samples or refreshments.)

• When wrapping up, announce that people can get started right away by getting together with the person who brought them.

• Allow time afterward to socialize.

Maximizing Your Meetings

• If more than one distributor is participating, discuss important points before the meeting so that everyone involved knows the agenda.

• Prepare and practice ahead of time what you will say, and encourage all the other speakers_to do the same. After you have spoken before groups many times, you'll be able to walk up in front of any group and speak with confidence.

• Have a visitor's sheet and ask attendees to sign in as they enter, so you can follow up with them.

• Put up a table with a display of the company products along with some empty product boxes to create an attractive visual presentation. Put out plenty of brochures, research studies, magazine articles, DVDs, product catalogs, and other handouts.

• Ask participating distributors to arrive fifteen minutes early to socialize and get comfortable. Studies show it takes at least fifteen minutes to get accustomed to being in an unfamiliar place.

• Have experienced distributors greet and interact with new attendees with friendly and assuring comments.

• Start and end meetings on time. Those who show up on time get a sense of professionalism. Latecomers will learn to be punctual.

• Schedule opportunity meetings weekly, so your group can rely on a regular day to get prospects to attend.

• Keep meetings less than an hour; thirty to forty-five minutes makes it easy for attendees to pay attention.

• Watch the faces and body language of those in your audience. If they are looking around or shifting in their seats, try asking a question to get people to interact or tell a humorous story to get people smiling and laughing.

Home Presentations

When carried out in your home, an opportunity meeting is often referred to as a "Private Business Reception." The PBR is a comfortable setting in which to introduce your program because of the safe at-home surroundings. The advantages of holding meetings in your home are that they

• Are fun to do and to attend;

• Provide a familiar, safe background;

• Are inexpensive to put on;

• Are convenient to attend;

• Can be planned on short notice;

• Are most likely to generate referrals;

• Are easy to do and to teach others to do.

If you choose to have opportunity meetings in your home, set up displays of your products visible and in easy reach throughout the house. Just as you would dress neatly for a meeting, clean and straighten up the yard to give the best impression.

Memorable Presentations

According to Chet Holmes, consultant to Fortune 100 companies, people retain 20 percent of what they see, 20 percent of what they hear, and 50 percent if they see and hear at the same time.

Without visual stimulation, the brain tunes in and out automatically—85 percent of all information is taken in through the eyes and 80 percent of all motivation is optically stimulated.

You will be far more memorable and motivating by using visual aids like storyboards, flip charts, or slides when making a presentation.

Another way to boost retention and liven up your presentation is to use humor. Humor can boost the retention of your message by 700 percent. Network marketing trainer, Tom "Big Al" Schreiter, is a master at getting people to laugh as they learn. See www.fortunenow.com.

To help audiences retain more from your talk, practice it enough out loud that you can repeat it easily and smoothly.

TACTIC 43. HOME PARTIES

Marketing through home parties has made companies like Tupperware and Avon household names. According to the Direct Selling Women's Alliance (www.mydswa.org.) party plan sales account for around $7 billion in direct selling revenues.

Informal and relaxed, home parties make a fun way for people to socialize and for you to introduce your products and opportunity in safe and friendly surroundings to several people at once. Best of all, they provide a venue to put immediate cash from sales into your hands.

In-home parties follow a simple outline with these basic steps or variations appropriate to your product:
• Ask the hostess to introduce you;
• Have satisfied customers give testimonials;
• Pass some products around the room;
• Describe key benefits while people are seeing, touching, smelling, tasting, or hearing about your products;
• Play a company DVD or video;
• Briefly recap key benefits on the DVD/video;
• Talk about different ways to use the product;
• Describe the business opportunity;

- Have a drawing for door prizes (everyone should get something;)
- Take orders.

It's no surprise that women dominate the party plan arena. Home parties are used to promote a wide variety of items women purchase, including household products, arts and crafts, toys, candles, cosmetics, jewelry, and many others. Lorna Rasmussen grew her PrePaid Legal organization through parties.

Party to the Rescue
by Lorna Rasmussen

My husband's major client declared that they would not be paying him, and my fledgling training business was making almost no money. So there I was, three weeks before Christmas, spending the last $600 we had to join a network marketing business. With no other options, I felt that this was my last best hope to save our family from bankruptcy. Besides, I had a son who still believed in Santa Claus. I had just three weeks to make it work.

But how, I wondered, does a professional person like me do this business? I had only worked in the traditional business world where the people I knew were used to calling on each other in their offices, not in homes and coffee shops.

Because it was December, holiday parties were in full swing. So I just began inviting people over to my house to "see" my new business and have some Christmas cookies. I had done a lot of networking for my training business and knew a lot of people in Atlanta. I simply started at the top of the list and worked my way down.

I would call and ask them if they would take a moment to look at some material about a new venture I had found. I would fax it over to them (this was 1994) and call back twenty minutes later to ask what they had liked best about what they saw. Those who were interested got an invitation to come over to my house and see a videotape presentation. My sponsor would be there to answer questions and sign people up.

A few months later, my seven-year-old son did a poster project in class and used what I was doing as his inspiration. It said "Like parties, like meetings? Join ____ and meet lots of people and have fun." That was really all we did. People were curious or polite enough to take a look. I never pressured them, I simply told them a compelling story, and before long I was earning enough to replace my husband's salary.

I believe that if you think first of the other person, give them value for the time they invest, and make it an enjoyable, non-pressured environment, this is an easy and very professional way to introduce business people to your MLM business. Relationships are created when you break bread with people (or share cookies), and it fosters an easy transition from the business world to the private world of home-based business.

I continue to this day to use versions of my "December blitz." One thing I love to do is to invite business people to lunch. It is billed as a networking lunch sponsored by my company. Everyone has a chance to introduce themselves and network, and then we do a short presentation on our business and services. Everyone feels they get a value out of attending because of the networking, but they also get enough information during the presentation to make a decision about our services or business opportunity.

By the way, I earned enough in my first three weeks in network marketing to give my son a great Christmas.

Lorna Rasmussen is a former small business owner and college professor who has become one of the most successful associates in her MLM business. She is also the author of the book The Absolute Best Way in the World for Women to Make Money, *available through* www.absolutebestway.com.

Getting referrals at home parties flows naturally. Guests are inquisitive about products and this interest makes it easy to ask if anyone else present would like to host a party.

Enliven your home parties with games, recipes and other tips on building a home party business, see www.homepartyplannetwork.com.

---

*"I am thankful for the mess to clean
after a party because it means I have
been surrounded by friends."*
~ Nancie J. Carmody ~

TACTIC 44. LEAD GROUP MEETINGS

Lead groups for networking help their members by referring each other's services. They offer a way of building relationships and expanding one's base of prospects. Before getting involved, be clear about how you will be able to help refer potential clients or suggest useful tactics to other members.

Participating in a networking group is a long-term social tactic, not an invitation to pitch your offer. After meeting your fellow members, make notes on their situation, so that when you come across a helpful resource, you can get it to them.

Follow up with members you can do something for. Make a warm impression by offering to get together over coffee or tea. People will be grateful, more likely to begin a networking relationship, and feel like reciprocating.

Be clear about the types of leads you are looking for in return. Are you looking for customers or for business builders? How do you define your ideal prospect? If you aren't sure, go back to your marketing plan and use the guidelines there to describe your perfect client, not only to yourself, but also to those who are willing to refer people to you.

After completing your marketing plan in Chapter 3, you should also now be able to give a concise and vivid account of your product or service so that you can quickly convey its benefits to your network.

To get the most out of networking groups, attend meetings regularly. Get to know the people involved. Show up with the intention to grow relationships and you'll find your group is ready to support you with referrals.

One of the largest referral groups with chapters across the U.S. is BNI at www.bni.com. Websites like www.linkedin.com offer the possibility of locating online networking opportunities as well.

TACTIC 45. SIZZLE SESSIONS

Sizzle sessions are informal meetings with distributors in small groups who talk about what's going on for them and brainstorm ideas for growth. Excited distributors getting together generate contagious energy. Don Failla says in his book, *The 45-Second Presentation That Will Change Your Life*, "Your network marketing program is the 'steak,' and everyone knows that the sizzle sells the steak!" Sizzle sessions are about creating the sizzle.

Unlike most other types of meetings, sizzle sessions are free-flowing chats about products, the comp plan, and how business is going for each person. These

Guerrilla Affirmation

I regularly play "outside the box" by using my *imagination* to find and create innovative marketing strategies that capture the attention of my customers and support my team members.

sessions help distributors feel they are connected as a team.

Checklist for this Chapter's Tactics

Place a check in the appropriate column for determining how or if you will use a tactic. Then return to your 7-sentence marketing plan - see Chapter 3 - and fill in the appropriate tactics in Step 4 of your plan.

Tactics In This Chapter	Using Well	Using, But Needs Work	Not Using	Not Right At This Time
41. Company Convention				
42. Opportunity Meetings				
43. Home Parties				
44. Leads Group Meetings				
45. Sizzle Sessions				

CHAPTER 11

TACTICS FOR PUBLIC EVENTS

"Every crowd has a silver lining."
~ Phineas Taylor Barnum ~

Fairs, expos, conventions, and trade shows get hordes of visitors over an intense couple of days, with attendees scouring display booths for new products and services. Public events provide a venue for you to demonstrate your item and gather feedback, prospective leads, and immediate cash sales.

Successful networkers who use shows as marketing tools have learned to find and exhibit at events that reach their target niche audience. They choose topic-centered events that draw prospects interested in that subject—people who are looking for products like theirs.

Putting yourself in the path of your ideal audience eases rapport building, lowers sales resistance, and positions you as a resource.

This chapter provides helpful ways to make the most of public events and helps you identify which types of events to choose for displaying your product, service, and opportunity. Topics covered in this chapter explore:

- Tips for maximizing results from public events
- Fairs, festivals and flea markets
- Consumer expos
- Using signs at events
- Using contests to gather leads

Before Events

Does the event have a theme? If so, does your product relate to it in a way you can build your display around?

Who attends the show? Will it be the general public or industry members? Why will people attend?

What size crowd is expected? Is this a first-time show (not usually recommended to display in) versus a known and well-publicized event?

Where is the show located? What are the dates and times? Will the event compete with other happenings, either locally or nationally?

How many other exhibitors will there be? Will other distributors in your company, but not in your line, have a display?

How much will the show cost? What expenses will you incur for booth rental, displays, travel, lodging, promotional materials, extra fees for union labor, promotion, and post-show follow-up?

Promote your show in advance by announcing events on your website and letting everyone in your group know about it. List your booth location and include a map to the event's location.

In the days leading up to an event, have your team set appointments to meet their prospects at the booth. The large crowds help convey the image that you represent a popular opportunity.

During Events

Get visitors to interact with you. By interacting with your booth's visitors, you can begin building rapport and getting people's permission to contact them later on after the event. Tips for inviting interaction include the offering of:

- Discount pricing for the time of the event;
- A free gift with purchase;
- A contest with a free prize;
- Free shipping on orders taken at the event.

One of your primary interaction strategies should be to get a prospect's contact information, especially an e-mail address, because this is the cheapest means for getting back with them. Offer to e-mail a special report or tip sheet so they will feel okay about sharing their address. Assure them that you won't share their contact information with others.

Have a team of distributors help with an event. Everyone involved gets a chance to interact with show attendees. Your team members can go around to the other booths and notice which displays attract the biggest crowds.

Start conversations with other exhibitors. You already know they are entrepreneurial-minded just because they are there.

"If you do build a great experience, customers tell each other about that."
~ Jeff Bezos ~

Keep Your Display Well Stocked

Whenever you do an exhibition or show, have a full display of items for sale. Studies show you'll sell more from a full display than a sparse one.

Hand Outs

Have a supply of products, samples, business cards, flyers, brochures, catalogs, article reprints, DVDs and other support materials neatly displayed on your table.

Offer free samples of your newsletter with consumer tips around the topic of the trade show.

Provide free coffee or drinks at a trade show and people will hang around your booth, which will attract others who figure something interesting is going on.

After Events

Keep track of how many new customers and distributors you signed up. Use the results of the event to motivate others in your organization.

Attendees will forget most of the booths they visited, so be sure to follow up with your leads and remind them you met them at the event. See Chapter 17 for ideas on how to do this.

TACTIC 46. FAIRS, FESTIVALS, AND FLEA MARKETS

Fairs and festivals draw large crowds seeking fun and enjoyable shopping venues. Examples include art and craft shows, renaissance fairs, historical theme shows, county and state fairs, and ethnic festivals. People wander among the colorful booths in the hope of discovering unique treasures.

Can your product be incorporated into craftwork? If so, you could create a huge backend business by marketing a unique craft item which you can use to then describe your MLM product. If not, partner with a craft artist to get a small display area in that individual's booth. Locate craft shows at www.craftmarketer.com/craft-shows.php.

If your product is edible, set up a booth at an ethnic theme festival or a renaissance show. Create a recipe booklet or offer prepared sample dishes.

Another and typically cheaper venue is flea markets. Tables are cheap and require little setup. Some flea markets are famous for drawing huge crowds, including the "First Monday" event in Canton, Texas or the San Jose Flea Market in California, which attracts 25,000 to 30,000 people every day.

"Treasure your relationships, not your possessions."
~ Anthony D'Angelo ~

TACTIC 47. CONSUMER EXPOS

According to *Tradeshow Week*, consumer trade shows or expos in the U.S. draw an average of close to 40,000 attendees each. Expos showcase all kinds of new products and services of interest to consumers.

Consumer expos are theme-based and draw people who are interested in topics as diverse as woodworking, prime-time living, babies, pets, homes, boats, gifts, cars, health, body-mind-spirit, weddings, computers, electronics, gardening, horses, and many others.

Job fair expos attract people who are looking for employment, but many attendees will also look at income opportunities.

As with consumer expos, industry trade shows provide venues for promoting new products in different industries. Many trade shows are produced by associations and industry groups. More than 13,000 industry trade shows attract 50 million plus visitors a year, according to Trade Show Exhibitors Association (TSEA.) To locate shows by industry, see www.tsnn.com and www.biztradeshows.com.

Trade Show Magic
By Margie Aliprandi

As a single mom with three little kids and a mortgage on a new home, there was no way I could make ends meet on my teacher's salary. I had a real and immediate need for income. Though I had a real stigma about network marketing, I found Neways and fell in love with their product.

I tried many systems and methods of prospecting simultaneously, but I soon discovered trade shows. Shows were fabulous because people came to me, I didn't have to go after them. Events worked well for me because my product was something that demonstrated easily—a natural nail gel system.

Trade shows are a great way to meet lots of interesting

people very quickly. Plus, shows make excellent venues for training new distributors. As they observe you interacting with show attendees, they learn the pitch, and by the end of the show they have developed knowledge, confidence, and can talk to anybody.

I did all kinds of events—big shows like at the Beauty Show at the Jacob Javitz Center in New York City and small local shows and boutiques. The shows I really liked were business-oriented trade shows, because the people attending were quite professional and there looking for a business. They would buy product as well, so they could determine how the product worked for them before starting a business. So it was a win from every angle.

One event stands out—it was a Christmas shopping show in Salt Lake City. We were demonstrating our nail system there. I was sitting with this one woman, holding her hand sculpting a nail for her. I told her, "You know, you would be so good at this business," and I started telling her where I saw this product going, how the company was positioned and how I felt about network marketing. She said she wasn't an impulse buyer and needed to think about it. About forty minutes later, she came back and bought a nail system at our retail price.

The next day, the woman returned and said, "Yesterday, you were talking about a business opportunity. Tell me what you mean." Not really knowing what I was doing—I didn't have an upline to advise me—I said, "Why don't you buy ten of these nail systems at wholesale and I will come and do a meeting in your home. Invite your friends, we'll demonstrate this for them. You'll easily pay off your credit card purchase before the end of this month and make a few hundred dollars for retail profit. And I'll be with you until all ten nail systems are sold."

She kind of reluctantly gave me her credit card and I kind of reluctantly took it and made the order. A few days later, she called me and said, "They're gone. I need to order more for the meeting!" So we then did a meeting at her house and she sold seven that night and three more the next day. She ordered ten again, and again. In her first full month in the business, counting the bonuses and her retail profit, my new distributor earned $5,200. With a story like that to tell, my business began growing leaps and bounds.

All of this allowed me to help her recruit and develop people within her sphere of influence. Sometimes we did two or three meetings in one night. I still earn today from the connections that came out of that Christmas show eighteen years ago.

For those just starting out, there are three things I recommend if you're considering trade shows.

First, do your due diligence about the show and negotiate for a booth that is well-located. Ask how many people attend, what kind of advertising do they do to get their crowds. Ask to talk to vendors from previous year's shows - those who offer products or services similar to yours. Ask them how they liked the event, how much traffic they got, how many sales they made, and what was their conversion rate for new distributors.

Secondly, have several clipboards with forms or questionnaires so everyone on your team can gather information at the same time. Offering a give-away of one or more of your products is a great way to entice people to share their information

Thirdly, get as much out of that face-to-face time while the person is there with you at the event. Get them enrolled, sell them some product, invite them to work the rest of the show with you and start training them right then and there - rather than trying to catch up with them after the show. By the end of the event, they'll be experts themselves.

Crown Diamond, Margie Aliprandi's organization, spans the globe. She is creator of the 1,000 Moms Making 1,000 Dollars and Making A Difference *campaign - empowering women worldwide with financial opportunity and grass roots education. Margie is also the author of the* Journey to Crown Diamond CD, *which outlines the ten principles to take you to the top of your pay plan. For a free copy, visit* www.MargieAliprandi.com/freeaudio

TACTIC 48. USING SIGNS AT EVENTS

Use signs when you display at an exhibition. A study showed that 94 percent of people taken through a given area recalled seeing a sign and 84 percent of those remembered the product and details of the offer. Add lighting on your sign for even better results. Sign advertising has been shown to boost sales by 54 percent, and when backlighting or motion is added, sales go up more than 100 percent.

TACTIC 49. BRINGING IN LEADS THROUGH CONTESTS

Speed your lead gathering at events with a contest. People leave their business card or fill out a card with their contact information in order to enter a drawing for a prize. The prize should be one of your products, so that anyone taking the time to enter is doing so because they are attracted to the benefits of your item. After the contest is over, contact the winner and ask where the prize should be delivered. Deliver it yourself, if possible, so you can learn more about the person and leave a brochure and order form for future orders. Mail a newsletter, brochure, CD or other promotional tool to all the other entries.

Fundraising events often include raffle contests. Donate one of your top products and attach a label with ordering instructions and your contact information on the container.

Guerrilla Affirmation

I leverage my time by looking for events where I can present my offer to hundreds of prospective customers and distributors.

Checklist for this Chapter's Tactics

Place a check in the appropriate column for determining how or if you will use a tactic. Then return to your 7-sentence marketing plan - see Chapter 3 - and fill in the appropriate tactics in Step 4 of your plan.

Tactics In This Chapter	Using Well	Using, But Needs Work	Not Using	Not Right At This Time
46. Fairs, Festivals, Flea Markets				
47. Consumer Expos				
48. Using Signs at Events				
49. Using Contests				

CHAPTER 12

TACTICS FOR USING E-MAIL

"The new information technology, Internet and e-mail, have practically eliminated the physical costs of communications."
~ Peter Drucker ~

In spite of the increase in unwanted spam e-mail, marketing through e-mail continues to generate sales. In a 2007 survey by Epsilon, it was found that 84 percent of e-mail users said they clicked through to read more about offers that had messages relevant to their needs. More than 70 percent said they bought because of an e-mail offer, and more than 50 percent forwarded e-mail messages about a product or service on to others.

Electronic communication is fast, cheap, and, when personalized, highly effective as a marketing tactic. This chapter gives you tips for promoting through:
- E-mail
- E-mail signatures
- Autoresponders
- Daily tips

TACTIC 50. E-MAIL

Personalized e-mails get better response. An example is an e-mail addressed to a person by first name in the e-mail subject area and with the person's name included in the body text of the e-mail. One study showed that personalized e-mails generated:

• Nearly 43 percent more click-throughs to a web page than non-personalized e-mail;
• Over 400 percent more sales on average than non-personalized e-mails;
• Almost 43 percent fewer unsubscribes (from a subscription list) than non-personalized e-mails.

Improve your response rates even more by letting people know in the e-mail subject area as well as in the opening text of the e-mail the reason you are writing to them.

People are busy, so get to the point of your message right away, whether it's letting them know about a special savings, a bonus incentive, or an event in their area. After you've made your reason clear, remind the reader of who you are and your previous relationship with them.

Send e-mail only to those people who have given you permission. When someone asks to be removed from your list, respond immediately. Don't get pegged as a spammer. You can lose your site and face criminal charges if found to be in violation of the CanSpam Act.

*"A spammer is like someone who stands
on a street corner, hands you an ad
circular, and then kicks you in the shins."*
~ Anonymous ~

E-mail Marketing Tips

• People get fewer e-mails in the afternoon, so yours will have a better chance of getting read when sent then.
• Avoid cramming your whole marketing message in a single e-mail. Make your note only as long as will

fit in single frame on the viewer's screen. Include a link to a web page with more details.

• A study by Lyris Technologies showed that e-mails not getting through to inboxes had less to do with spam filters and more to do with the content. A big factor in whether e-mails got through was heavy use of images, which causes spam scores to go up. ISPs block incoming e-mails when users complain, so it's critical that you keep your message relevant, simple, and clean.

• One study showed a higher number of sales when an e-mail offer arrived on Friday.

E-mail Signatures

One of the most overlooked yet opportune ways to promote your offer is exploiting the bottom of your e-mails in an area known as the e-mail signature. It's free ad space and it works.

Most e-mail management programs allow you to create a variety of e-mail signatures that automatically appear at the conclusion of your e-mail message. This area is like the P.S. of a letter—and it may end up being read more often than the body of your e-mail.

Create different signatures for different categories of communications, like a special message for distributors and another for prospects. Include a persuasive testimonial by a satisfied customer or research study. E-mail signatures make an ideal two-step marketing tactic. Your signature will (step 1) entice a click-through to a web address, which (step 2) provides more details.

---

*"Electronic communication is an instantaneous
and illusory contact that creates a sense of intimacy without
the emotional investment that leads to close friendships."*
~ Clifford Stoll ~

Autoresponders

Autoresponders are automated e-mails, programmed to deliver immediate or scheduled replies to anyone who sends an e-mail to the autoresponder address. E-mail autoresponder addresses appear just like any other kind of e-mails. For example, someone sending e-mail to welcome@yourdomain.com could receive a programmed welcome message from you, which could link to a web page with a promotional offer.

Autoresponders help you leverage your time by automating the process of answering commonly asked questions. Autoresponders go out immediately and the receiver gets it as fast as he receives any other e-mails.

Autoresponders can include a series of messages. For instance, you can program an autoresponder series to deliver a mini-course in how to save on legal expenses for your small business. Or, you can deliver issues of a newsletter via an autoresponder series.

Autoresponders are easy to set up. Providers allow you to create messages, schedule their delivery time, send the e-mails, and provide links for those who wish to stop receiving (opt out) your announcements. You can also view and export your list of subscribers.

Many web hosts provide autoresponder services for free. If yours does not, there are free and paid autoresponder providers. A disadvantage of using a free service is that these services make their money by selling advertising to others whose message is included on every e-mail that goes out from you. This means your prospects see someone else's product offer as well as yours.

Although using a free service may be tempting, you'll get better response by delivering only your own messages. A paid service can cost anywhere from $10 to $50 per month. Examples of paid autoresponder services providers include www.aweber.com and www.getresponse.com.

Tactic 51. Daily Tips

For almost any topic, you can probably find plenty of interesting information you can break up into bite-sized nuggets of wisdom, which can go into an autoresponder series to deliver "daily tips" to your customers, distributors, or prospects.

Not only will these tips help your contacts, you add to your own knowledge by doing product and market research and accumulating data that can be incorporated in your other marketing approaches.

Take any useful content (that isn't copyrighted) about your product or its ingredients and benefits. Your tip-of-the-day (or week) series can be a free service or you can charge for a year's subscription.

Daily tips help your customers and distributors find out more ways to use a product than they knew about before. Invite subscribers to submit their own product tip stories and credit them by name.

Make your daily tips helpful—not sales pitches. Let your marketing message or link reside in your e-mail signature to refer readers to your website for more information and to order products.

Checklist for this Chapter's Tactics

Place a check in the appropriate column for determining how or if you will use a tactic. Then return to your 7-sentence marketing plan - see Chapter 3 - and fill in the appropriate tactics in Step 4 of your plan.				
Tactics In This Chapter	Using Well	Using, But Needs Work	Not Using	Not Right At This Time
50. E-mail				
51. Daily Tips				

CHAPTER 13

WEB MARKETING TACTICS

"True interactivity is not about clicking on icons or downloading files, it's about encouraging communication."
~ Edwin Schlossberg ~

Your website can help you get your marketing message to the world 24 hours a day, 7 days a week, 365 days a year, at an average cost of between $70 to $300 per year. Few other promotional venues provide equal potential for exposure at such a low cost.

The Internet is a tool for zeroing in on those most likely to buy your product. For example, Jupiter Research reported that, in 2006, 54 million people in the U.S. connected to content created online about health and wellness issues.

Whether you promote a program related to travel, kitchen accessories, legal aid, or skin care, search engines daily serve up links to thousands of websites to people looking for services like yours.

If your target audience is baby boomers, you'll be happy to know that a survey from Third Age Inc. showed 73 percent of adults age 45 said their top online activity was shopping. And 96 percent of boomers reported they would pass on product or service information to friends.

The Internet can automate your lead gathering, generate product sales, and help you train distributors faster. But it can also tempt you into sacrificing relationship-building for speed and numbers.

This chapter shows you how to attract more people online, inspire their trust, and encourage them to interact with you. Learn how to grow your warm list online through:

- A website (your own and/or a personalized company replicated site)
- Incoming links
- Online articles
- Pay-per-click
- Pay-per-call
- Audio/Video downloads
- Blogging
- Podcasting
- Newsgroups and forums

TACTIC 52. WEBSITE

Many MLMs provide distributors paid or free personalized corporate web pages. These pages are usually replicated and approved content offering visitors access to a shopping catalog and a business opportunity presentation. You can link to your company pages by links sent out in e-mail, in ad copy, or through links on other sites you own.

If your parent company doesn't restrict you from doing so, you can create your own domain name site with educational content focused around your product or service. Since you can add unique content, your private domain site stands a better chance of getting indexed and ranked in search engine queries than replicated content pages from your company, because search engines tend to ignore pages with duplicate content already showing up online. Check your company's policies and procedures about private websites.

Here are three compelling reasons for why you should make use of a website to promote your offer:

- More than 330,000,000 people worldwide were

using the Internet as of March, 2007, according to Nielsen.

• Online retail sales in 2006 topped $102 billion.

• Of 7,000 consumers interviewed in a 2005 BIGresearch survey, 75 percent reported they regularly or sometimes research products online before going to a store to make a purchase.

There is a clear opportunity for network marketers to provide website content facilitating consumer research, which, in turn, opens the door to delivering personalized attention and fast delivery of products.

A website helps you cater to your market. A site can provide helpful articles, research studies, breaking news, special offers, scheduled newsletters, convenient shopping, and multiple ways of contacting you.

"If you have a web site, it makes your small business look big."
~ Natalie Sequera ~

Getting Found by Search Engines

Registering a domain name and putting content on your site does not guarantee that search engines will display your pages in search query results. There are multiple factors that contribute to getting found by the search engines, including the presence of:

• Useful, relevant content for your readers
• Keyword phrases in your text related to your topic
• Keywords in your HTML meta title tag
• Keywords in heading tags
• Images named with your keywords
• Linked text with your keywords

- Number and authority of links coming into your site
- Text of links coming into your site
- Topic consistency throughout your site
- Number of pages on your site.

According to a SEOmoz report, there are also things you must avoid doing at the risk of being excluded from search engine indexing, such as:

- Being hosted on a server with intermittent access
- Having duplicate or very similar content on your own site or content copied from other sites
- Linking from your site to sites banned by the search engines for spam or other reasons
- Getting involved in link schemes to artificially boost your rankings
- Having duplicate meta title tags on the pages of your site.

There are too many elements of SEO (search engine optimization) to cover here, but the Internet is loaded with tutorials and courses to teach you more. See the article for network marketers at www.gmmlm.com/net/.

The Power of the Web
How James' Group Multiplied Fast Online

My group was growing, but it was at an agonizingly slow pace. One day, I was following up with a new second-level distributor, only to hear him tell me, "I am not interested in this as a business; please don't call me again. I'll just buy the product wholesale." I understood how he felt, because I originally resisted getting involved in network marketing myself, so I left him alone.

A couple of months later, I heard from his sponsor,

who was a good friend, that his distributor was going to be in the same town, around the same time as a talk by the scientist who developed the product he had signed up for. Despite his earlier request to leave him alone, I took a chance and e-mailed him about the event.

He thanked me, went to the presentation, met the scientist in person, and got so excited that he put up a website to promote the product. Drawing on his background of creating websites, this fellow used the Internet to bring in almost 500 customers and distributors in his first year, and another 600 the next year.

His site became popular because he had pages with useful content that ranked high in search engine query results for keywords related to the product. Other distributors were mailing out tapes by the thousands, which spurred a lot of Internet search, which led visitors to find his site.

Even though, like me, he had initially proclaimed a firm "no" to the business, he jumped in readily when he saw he could use his existing skills building websites to grow a successful income.

Tactic 53. Incoming Links

Part of your online campaign for traffic should include getting links from popular sites with content on topics similar to yours.

The number and quality of links pointing to your site remains high among the factors influencing getting ranked in the search engines for your keywords. The linking text in incoming links is critical, because it tells the search engines your site is relevant for those keywords.

For example, if you choose to rank number one in Google results for "natural skin care products," that will require more sites linking to your site with the link text phrase "natural skin care products" than the current number one listing in search results.

---

*"The message for business people
contemplating their place in cyberspace
is simple and direct: get linked or get lost."*
~ Vic Sussman and Kenan Pollack ~

Think of your site as a person with a message who is attempting to get noticed among a crowd of people shouting similar messages. Getting noticed (ranking high in the search engines) will have a lot to do with what authorities (popular websites) say about the person (your site.) In the same way, it is what other sites say about yours that makes your site a credible reference in the eyes of the search engines.

However, be sure to vary incoming link text, because search engines like Google are sophisticated enough to know when you are trying to artificially boost your rankings with too many incoming links with the same text. If you are seen to be "link spamming," you risk being banned from search results.

Tactic 54. Online Articles

For search engines to index your site, they must find text or content. Original articles are a great way to satisfy the requirement for useful content. The more text on your site, the more words will get indexed and referenced by the search engines.

Articles written on topics and containing keywords related to your product or service help your rankings by adding "weight" and relevancy. Not only will articles on your own pages help your site gain authority around a specific subject, articles on other sites linking to yours will boost your rankings, too. Links from other sites to yours, appearing within articles (except for duplicate content) are viewed by the search engines as natural links and, therefore, a boost to your site's relevancy.

There are many article depository sites online where you can post your own articles or find free articles to post on your site. Just do a search for "article directory" or "article sites."

The problem with using articles freely available is that, because they contain duplicated content, the search engines tend to ignore them when calculating rank. However, fresh original content does count. Just remember to include lots of words and phrases related to your topic.

TACTIC 55. PAY-PER-CLICK

You can rank #1 for your search terms in Google's Adwords (www.adwords.google.com) in ten minutes or less. You'll pay for the position, but people do click on and buy from what are called pay-per-click ads.

Pay-per-click programs allow merchants to position brief text ads that show up next to organic search engine query results. For an example, type in "legal services" at Google and you will see pay-per-click ads off to the right, under "Sponsored Links." Each time an Internet user clicks on an ad, the merchant who wrote and paid for the ad pays for each click. The cost-per-click is determined by a complex formula that includes an auction process. Merchants bid to place #1, or whatever rank they choose. In general, the more popular the keyword phrase, the higher the cost-per-click.

However, paying for the top position is not necessarily the smartest move. Your competitors may click on your ads in an effort to drive you out by running up your costs. A study by Click Forensics showed pay-per-click fraud is close to 15 percent.

Experts seem to agree that the #3 position is a better investment. Since competition for ad position is a factor in the costs you pay per click, the third place position is usually dramatically cheaper than the number one spot and there are fewer incidents of fraudulent clicks.

Google Adwords, Yahoo Search Marketing, and MIVA rank at the top of the list of pay-per-click programs, according to a site that reviews pay-per-click providers (www.payperclicksearchengines.com.)

With pay-per-clicks, like any type of paid advertising, you should test small limited campaigns before investing money in larger ad runs.

Tactic 56. Pay-Per-Call

Pay-per-call ads work similar to pay-per-clicks, except your ad prompts viewers to phone you. You only pay for calls actually generated.

Like pay-per-click ads, the cost of a pay-per-call ad is decided by advertisers bidding on keyword phrases. The more popular a keyword phrase, the higher the cost-per-call. The highest bidding ad earns the top position in search results.

Speaking with your customer live is worth more to you than getting them to click through to a web page. You know they are interested, because they are calling. According to merchants running pay-per-call campaigns, conversions can be 50 percent higher when

Guerrilla Affirmation

I never send bulk e-mails or spam, but I do use e-mail to stay in touch with customers and team members because it costs nothing and it keeps my name in their minds.

you can answer questions about your products, learn about your customer's situation, and initiate person-to-person relationships.

Service providers of pay-per-call ads include: www.ingenio.com, www.estara.com, www.jambo.com.

TACTIC 57. AUDIO/VIDEO DOWNLOADS

Make your site worth talking about by adding audio or video clips. More and more sites now include brief audio clips to enrich user experience. Increasing broadband availability and Internet improvements have made it easier to record and publish audio clips to your site.

Video enhances response. Studies from the National Association of Broadcasters, DoubleClick, and others show that streaming video generates double the clickthrough rates of banner ads.

Consider services such as VM Direct at www.yourbusinessvideos.com, which offers video mail at under $10 a month, along with the ability to do webcasting, pay-per-view broadcasts, have password-protected sites, and feast on a host of other goodies.

Google bought YouTube for $1.65 billion, a signal of where online video is headed. Many of the popular video sites allow you to embed your video clip in a blog, giving you even more possibilities for presenting a multimedia message. People retain more of a message when it's presented in stimulating ways.

TACTIC 58. BLOGGING

Blogs are another way to get your fresh content online fast. Search engines love fresh content; blog pages often rank high in Google search results.

Blogging is a way to express yourself without editing, an instant way to get published, a journal from which to sprout news, and a way to create community. It's also a way to create new customers, because people who read your blog get to know you as a human being rather than a marketer.

"I believe that this notion of self-publishing, which is what Blogger and blogging are really about, is the next big wave of human communication."
~ Eric Schmidt, CEO Google ~

Blogging is increasingly popular. Through building or posting to websites and blogs, 53 million U.S. Internet users now contribute content expressing their thoughts and resource links, according to *The Virtual Handshake: Opening Doors and Closing Deals Online*, by David Teten and Scott Allen.

If you are going to blog, be ready to add content regularly. When you are low on ideas, search for copyright- free articles, news feeds, and highpoints from news sites to add to your blog. You can also include product reviews.

TACTIC 59. PODCASTING

Podcasts are digitally recorded audio files that can be downloaded from websites onto personal computers or listening devices such as iPods or MP3 players.

As a marketing tool, you can podcast your own radio show, list it online in podcast directories, and promote it as an educational audio. It just takes a fairly up-to-date computer, a microphone, and a topic you love talking about.

A survey reported by *The Guardian* (UK) showed 80 percent of podcast listeners said they were likely to seek more information on products or services when they heard about them on a podcast.

Podcasting allows you to communicate directly with your target market. You can create subscriptions so that subscribers automatically receive your new podcasts as you publish them.

Use podcasting to explain product benefits, which increases customer loyalty. Stand out from the competition by using a podcast to explore new trends in your field.

Ready to podcast? Just Google the phrase "create podcast" and check out the many evolving tools for creating and uploading your audio files. Listen to the podcast on marketing with podcasts at http:// radio.weblogs.com/0144135/.

TACTIC 60. NEWSGROUPS AND FORUMS

Newsgroups, discussion groups, and forums allow readers to communicate about a mutually interesting topic. Groups draw members seeking feedback on subjects such as weight loss, diabetes, ice hockey, alcohol recovery, travel overseas, and just about any other topic you can think of.

According to the book, *The Virtual Handshake,* 84 percent of Internet users in the U.S. have gone online to get information from an online group.

Discussion groups fall into two categories— moderated and unmoderated. If the group is unmoderated, you typically find postings that are nothing more than ads. Moderated groups, however, are managed by someone who watches postings to weed out spam ads.

You can join as many groups as you have time to keep up with. Check new messages day to day and you will find many opportunities to answer individuals who ask questions or share problems. Build relationships with people by offering advice as a helpful expert in your field. The idea is to be recognized for being of service.

Discussion groups are not the place to blatantly promote your product or opportunity. If you do this, you'll be asked to leave or be blocked from posting.

However, most groups do allow the use of e-mail signatures.

Posting on forums and newsgroups can create business for you down the road, because once the members come to know and trust you, they are more likely to read your e-mail signature and click through to your website to learn more about you.

Locate discussion groups in your subject at:

http://groups.google.com

http://groups.yahoo.com

http://groups.msn.com

http://groups.aol.com

http://squidoo.com/groups/

If you've searched and still can't find a group around your topic, start your own. The sites listed above allow you to set up and run your own group.

Advertise your opportunity for free at:

finance.groups.yahoo.com/group/directsellingdirectory/

www.directsaleswomen.com/free_advertising.

For sites through which to network with direct sales reps in your field, see

www.directsellingbusiness.com/business_groups.

Tactic 61. Social Networking Sites

Business people are flocking to social networking sites to grow their personal networks. eMarketer reported that social network sites would earn around $865 million in 2007 from advertising.

Networking sites like Ryze (www.ryze.com) and others have proven useful to help people grow their networks for business or career advancement. Members upload photos, news, and personal profiles, and connect with each other by adding friends, which can lead to meeting friends of friends. Even the rich and famous, including Bill Gates, have registered on www.LinkedIn.com, a social networking site for business owners.

By setting up a profile on a social networking site, you can write about your personal life in all the detail you wish. You can discuss products you have found beneficial. You can link to your main website which provides more details and a shopping cart for placing orders.

Ryze members get a free networking-oriented home page and can send messages to other members. They can also join special networks related to their industry, interests, or location. Examples of networks on Ryze useful for listing MLM opportunities include:

- Direct Selling Network
  www.dsnetwork-network.ryze.com
- Entrepreneur's Network
  www.entrepreneurs-network.ryze.com
- Promote It Network
  www.promoteit-network.ryze.com

To locate more social networks, search for "social networking sites" at www.google.com.

Tactic 62. Online Classifieds

Millions of people read online classifieds. The largest online classified site, www.craigslist.org, attracted almost 14 million visitors in July, 2006—almost a 100 percent increase over the same time the previous year.

At the time of this writing, posting an ad at Craigslist is free. Target where your ad displays by city—a great way to line up local prospects you can meet face to face. You can include your actual contact information, or you can let Craigslist send you e-mail responses anonymously to protect your real e-mail address. One strategy is to list individual items for sale in a classified ad and then link to your personalized corporate website with a complete catalog. You can make multiple postings, but you will have to change your ad copy. Be sure to read the rules for posting.

More online classified sites include:
www.classifieds.com
www.livedeal.com
www.dominionenterprises.com/OurBusinesses.html

---

*"The Internet is just a world passing
around notes in a classroom."*
~ Jon Stewart ~

TACTIC 63. SPYING

Spying is another word to describe doing research on
your competition. Go online to research companies and
distributors in your topic area. Get ideas for improving
your strategies from the movers and shakers. Spying
is essential because it:

- Tells you what's new in your field;
- Tells you who's making the news;
- Gives you knowledge of competing products;
- Instills confidence in your customers and group
when you can reveal breaking trends;
- Identifies potential fusion marketing partners.

Visit your competitors' websites. Is it clear what
their offer is? Is it easy to order? Is the site easy to
navigate? Can you find exactly what you are seeking?

Buy something from a competitor. See how their
shopping cart handles your transaction. Did it go
smoothly? Did the product ship right away? Did anyone
follow-up with you about your experience? Was the
order person friendly and enthusiastic?

If your competition isn't providing awesome service
to its customers, you can emphasize areas in which you

excel in your marketing as a benefit to doing business with your company.

Checklist for this Chapter's Tactics

Place a check in the appropriate column for determining how or if you will use a tactic. Then return to your 7-sentence marketing plan - see Chapter 3 - and fill in the appropriate tactics in Step 4 of your plan.				
Tactics In This Chapter	Using Well	Using, But Needs Work	Not Using	Not Right At This Time
52. Website				
53. Incoming Links				
54. Online Articles				
55. Pay-Per-Click				
56. Pay-Per-Call				
57. Audio/Video Downloads				
58. Blogging				
59. Podcasting				
60. Newsgroups and Forums				
61. Social Networking Sites				
62. Online Classifieds				
63. Spying				

CHAPTER 14

GETTING PEOPLE TO CALL YOU

---

*"Shoot for the moon. Even if you
miss, you'll land among the stars."*
~ Les Brown ~

One of the most advantageous positions you can have is to get referrals by becoming an expert resource. As an author or teacher, people will seek you out for advice and refer others to you.

You don't have to compete with celebrities to become an expert in your arena. By identifying and targeting a niche subject, you can become the recognized resource people turn to for advice. In addition to allowing you opportunities to describe your network marketing offer, you can earn money writing and selling books and articles, teaching seminars, consulting, and in other ways as well.

Most marketing is *push-energy*; you push your message toward people, hoping for response. Getting people to call you is *pull-energy*; it's typically less costly. People seek out experts for answers and tend to treat them with respect.

Let's say you are a distributor for an online travel agency. Become the expert on Belize or Fuji or the Grand Canyon by writing booklets, creating a popular website, offering free information by phone, and getting articles published. Your travel service becomes a natural fit for people who find you for insider tips on visiting those places.

This chapter teaches you six ways to position yourself as an expert:

1. Writing articles
2. Writing a book
3. Getting free publicity
4. Teaching adult education courses
5. Public speaking
6. Listing yourself as an expert online.

What It Means to Be an Expert

• Determine a specific topic or niche based on your life experiences or interests.

• Increase your familiarity with the subject through reading books, newsletters, magazines; joining associations; networking through Internet discussion groups; and keeping up with trends in your field.

• Create a bio or resume listing your experience, credentials, degrees, endorsements, published articles and books, previous media appearances, public speaking engagements, seminars, awards, consultant projects, and a sheet that includes client testimonials.

• Produce a newsletter, column, articles and a website, make public appearances or present workshops, and use all other means you may have of gathering a mailing list of people who have read, seen, or heard about you or your material.

• Within your specialty, become a consultant and establish appropriate fees for counseling individuals or businesses.

"An expert is a person who has made all the mistakes that can be made in a very narrow field."
~ Niels Bohr ~

• Design a brochure, business card, website, stationery and logo to brand yourself and create name recognition.

• Learn how to do radio and TV interviews that result in sales for your books.

• Become a paid speaker.

• Conduct classes, workshops, and seminars on your subject.

• Host your own cable TV or radio show.

• Write and publish articles for major magazines.

• Write and syndicate a magazine, newspaper and Internet column.

• Write books, special reports, and newsletters to sell at public appearances and workshops. Create audio CDs and video presentations on DVDs.

• Get endorsed by organizations and trade associations in your field.

How to Become an Expert in Your Field
by Barbara Brabec

The words you use to describe what you do (your title) are a powerful positioning tool that has much to do with the kind of customers and clients you will attract.

For example, when I began my business, I called myself a "crafts marketing authority" because I began as a crafts seller, then went on to write a crafts marketing book and publish a related newsletter. Initially, I attracted creative people only.

With the publication of the first edition of by book, *Homemade Money*, however, I had a product with a market much broader than the crafts industry. To tap it, I had to reposition myself and my business in the eyes of book buyers, and I did this by first changing the name of my business from "Artisan Crafts" to "Barbara Brabec Productions" so I could build credibility for my name. Then I changed the name of the newsletter I was then publishing from *Sharing Barbara's Mail* to *National Home Business Report*. Finally, I changed what I called myself. Not just "an author of home-business books," but a "Home Business Development Specialist." (I was the first one in the United States to use this title, but others soon picked up on it.)

In total, this repositioning move greatly broadened my market, increased my sales, and made my name better known, all of which, in turn, enhanced my reputation as an expert and enabled me to command higher speaking fees. Not bad for just changing a few words here and there.

In describing what you do, remember that what you do isn't necessarily what you *do*. In the years when I was writing and publishing my own books, producing a newsletter, speaking at conferences and presenting home-business seminars, what I was actually *doing* was "helping people succeed in a home-based business" (my "core concept statement"). Today, even though my activities are different, I'm still helping people succeed in their home-based endeavors, but my client base has now been expanded to include designers, writers and self-publishers.

You may not feel like an expert now, but you may wake up one morning and find you are one. If so, don't be afraid to let others know because media folks *love* experts. "Experts 'happen' quickly," said Art Spikol in one of his *Writer's Digest* columns. "One day you're an ordinary person who knows a lot of big things about something little or a lot of little things about something big. The next day you're quoted somewhere. Before the next 24 hours go by, you're an expert."

Barbara Brabec has been working with and writing about home-based entrepreneurs since 1971. She is one of America's best-known home-business authors. See www.BarbaraBrabec.com.

Tactic 64. Write Articles for Publications

Instead of putting out money on advertising venues that have little credibility anyway, go for free publicity through writing articles. Where a book review might give you a paragraph or two of mention, feature articles may run two or more full pages. If you were to buy two pages of advertising space in most major magazines, the cost could run $20,000 to $50,000 or more.

In addition to the free exposure, all major magazines and many other print publications pay authors for content. As an expert in your subject, you have knowledge or access to information that is of interest to special audiences.

Read recent issues of publications your prospective customers buy. Learn what kind of topics they cover and how current news might relate to your expertise to give you ideas for articles to submit to editors. A good story helps fill a publication's ongoing necessity for fresh material.

Keep a log of every place you get an article in print. Use your list to build a resume of where you've been published because this will help establish your authority on a subject.

Locate magazines and newspapers on any subject or in any geographical region by doing an online search for "media directory."

Tactic 65. Write a Book

Write and publish a book and gain immediate respect. Book authors get invited to teach and speak—both of which can earn money.

You may wonder what writing has to do with network marketing. Not much, at first glance. But authorship opens doors and gives you credibility, which provides leverage to communicate with larger and larger groups of people. Network marketing is a "people business," and writing a book is a good way to attract attentive prospects.

If you aren't inclined to write a book, you can still be an author by hiring a ghostwriter or freelance writer to compose manuscripts for you. To locate freelance writers willing to work by the project, see www.elance.com or www.guru.com.

When editors and producers seek experts, they often turn to book authors. One of the most frequently searched directories for expert sources is Radio-TV Interview Report, www.rtir.com, a provider of paid listings to the media.

TACTIC 66. FREE PUBLICITY (PR)

Many MLM companies prohibit distributors from seeking publicity on their own and require all publicity copy to be approved before publishing. However, as the author of a book, special report, or interview, you may be able to garner free publicity for your own information product without involving the parent company.

It can take as little as a one-page news release to publicize your expertise which then mentions your information product (book, CD, newsletter, etc.) A news release can make your book appear as an authoritative source.

Most people have become immune to advertisements, yet they continue to read news articles appearing in magazines or newspapers to stay up to date with what's happening.

Newspapers, magazines, radio and TV editors and producers have an ongoing demand for newsworthy and entertaining content to their readers.

Have you ever wondered how it is that there is always just enough news to fit in the current issue of *Time* magazine or in your daily paper? Experts say that approximately 75 percent of everything we read in periodicals is placed PR.

Learn how to write a news release by studying headlines and articles appearing in publications your target audience reads. Submit yours to sites such as www.prweb.com and www.prnewswire.com. One study showed that 90 percent of journalists begin story research by searching online.

James Dillehay Explains What Editors Look For

As a former magazine editor and publisher, I received a steady flow of submitted articles from wannabe published writers every week.

I could always tell a novice writer from a pro. The new writer wrote to promote herself or her product. It was obvious she hadn't taken time to read our back issues before submitting her manuscripts.

Those whose stories did get published had clearly read my magazine first and knew what our reader focus was. They produced useful tips and resourceful content our audience could put to immediate use. They made my job easier, so I was happy to provide them with the PR value of getting their stories in print.

TACTIC 67. TEACH ADULT EDUCATION COURSES

Teaching classes and seminars can be a lucrative way of reaching new audiences eager to learn. Assuming you deliver a good presentation, you gain immediate respect as an authoritative resource.

Teaching classes provides a venue for you to meet more people with whom you can eventually build relationships. In addition to getting paid for presenting courses to audiences, teachers can sell their books, CDs, and videos at the back of the room.

One way to find appropriate teaching opportunities is to create a list of community college continuing education programs, associations, clubs, trade organizations, trade shows, conventions, community events, corporations and businesses related to your topics. All of these offer ongoing educational opportunities to their constituents.

Avoid using classes as a sales pitch; instead, offer quality advice around a topic in which you have some expertise. Make yourself available for follow up through a newsletter or coaching. People will contact you for advice.

For a guide to classes and teaching venues on hundreds of subjects, see www.shawguides.com. For online class venues, see www.universalclass.com.

TACTIC 68. PUBLIC SPEAKING

Public speaking, like teaching, positions you as an expert and rewards you with the respect of your audiences. Typically, public speaking events will draw many times more people than classes and workshops.

Speakers are looked upon as authorities and attract queries from their audiences, which then opens the door to making connections.

Speaking to groups may feel intimidating at first, but with a little practice, can grow into an enjoyable and energizing experience. A safe way to get comfortable making public talks is through Toastmasters. You can practice speaking before small groups, get feedback from members and other speakers, and enjoy meeting new people who might sign up for your newsletter, invite you to present at their business event, or join you in your network marketing business. To locate a chapter of Toastmasters near you, see www.toastmasters.org.

"Remember that you are a teacher, you are helping people, making them feel safer, taking them from fear to love, from ignorance to knowledge."
~ Stuart Wilde ~

Read *Speak and Grow Rich* by Dottie Walters. Dottie is the guru of public speaking, and her book is a step-by-step guide to making money by opening your mouth.

To help prepare yourself for speaking and presenting for money, see the free articles at www.antion.com/freear~1.htm. To get speaking jobs, register yourself as an expert with speaker agencies like those listed at www.speakers.com and www.speaking.com.

Tactic 69. Be an Expert Online

Several websites provide opportunities to list your expertise. As a registered authority, you will receive questions from people looking for free advice on a given topic which you can reply to directly. Your e-mail signature can promote your newsletter, website, article archives, e-books, seminars or network marketing products. Sites to list yourself as an expert:

www.askanexpert.com
www.allexperts.com
www.suite101.com
www.about.com
www.authorsandexperts.com

See www.profnet.com, a service of PR Newswire which, for a subscription fee, allows you to list yourself as an expert in their database, which is searched 10,000 times per month by journalists looking for authoritative sources to interview or quote in articles.

A positive side effect of giving out expert advice is that you may get asked questions for which you'll have to expand your own knowledge to answer. Learning about your audience helps you strengthen your credibility and discovering new ways to help them.

Teleseminars

Teleseminars provide a way to get the word out about your product or opportunity to large audiences in an interactive format. Teleseminars are convenient for you because they can be conducted from your home phone or cell phone. Attendees call into a designated number with a pass code you have sent them. Calls can be educational and/or entertaining. Listeners often choose to follow up to get more information, making teleseminars an effective marketing tactic.

You can interview experts, tape the calls and create CDs you can sell or give away later (be sure to get permissions from everyone you interview on the call.)

With increased costs of travel, teleseminars are gaining in appeal. You can even set up calls for free through services like www.freeconference.com.

Checklist for this Chapter's Tactics

Place a check in the appropriate column for determining how or if you will use a tactic. Then return to your 7-sentence marketing plan - see Chapter 3 - and fill in the appropriate tactics in Step 4 of your plan.				
Tactics In This Chapter	Using Well	Using, But Needs Work	Not Using	Not Right At This Time
64. Write Articles for Publications				
65. Write a Book				
66. Free Publicity				
67. Teach Adult Education Classes				
68. Public Speaking				
69. Be an Expert Online				

CHAPTER 15
TACTICS FOR ADVERTISING

"A good advertisement is one which sells the product without drawing attention to itself."
~ David M. Ogilvy ~

It's a common misunderstanding that marketing is advertising, but advertising is only ONE of the 100 ways in this book on how to market your offer.

Advertising costs money, but gives you control of what your message says, when your ad appears, where it is published, how often it repeats, and who your message reaches.

This book is loaded with both free marketing tactics and those that cost money. While you may not yet have a budget for paid advertising, there will come a day when your compensation check provides you with surplus income. Investing the extra cash into ad campaigns for growing your business can be a vehicle for momentum-like growth.

Be aware that an effective ad program via any or all of the methods described in this chapter can bring in scores or even hundreds of leads every week. So before you advertise, think about how many new recruits you can realistically give attention to. If you can't build rapport with every lead, new people will leave just as fast as they arrive and your ad dollars will have been wasted.

Ads will be more cost-effective when you choose publications and other media whose audience matches your target group. For instance, advertise beauty and skin care products to readers of women's beauty magazines or a list of skin care product buyers, not in a publication for cat lovers.

This chapter helps you learn about advertising to readers most likely to show interest in your offer through:

- Calendar of events listings
- Direct mail
- Card decks
- Inserts and ride-alongs
- Display ads
- Classified ads in print media
- Free offers
- Co-op ads
- Your car as an ad

Here's how to use strategic goals to maximize your results with any ad campaign you run, regardless of the media in which your ads appear:

- Have a goal of what you choose to achieve from paid advertising. Know how many new leads you can support.
- Set a budget of how much money you are willing to invest in advertising over the next year.
- One-time ads rarely work. Don't invest money in paid advertising unless you are prepared to run a campaign long enough to generate measurable responses—at least 8 to 9 times over a year.
- Keep control of your ad campaigns by focusing on only one or two media at a time. If you have too many projects running concurrently, it's easy to get your results confused.

"In general, my children refused to eat anything that hadn't danced on TV."
~ Erma Bombeck ~

• Before paying standard rates for ads in print publications, inquire about remnant space or "white space." Check the publication's ad deadline date and inquire about unsold space with them on or near their deadline. Be sure your ad copy is ready to send at a moment's notice.

• When investing money in advertising, remember to test. Always start small and test your results before putting more money into an ad campaign. Track and measure your results.

• Repeat ads that get results; change or drop ads that don't.

• Double check your ad copy for grammatical or typographical errors. Remember to include your contact information and a call to action, telling the reader exactly what you would have them do.

• Most MLM and direct selling companies have policies about advertising. Your ad's content will require approval by your company, so go through the proper channels before investing money in paid advertising.

Tactic 70. Calendar of Events Listings

Many daily newspapers, magazines, and free community newspapers provide a calendar of upcoming events. List your opportunity meeting, home party, or open house reception at a cost much less than you would pay for a display ad.

Readers scour calendar of event listings for interesting things to do. They perceive an event listing as news, not as an ad. It's easy for readers to mark their own calendar with your event because listings are usually formatted like calendars.

Check out the racks of free publications found near the exits of many grocery stores for potential magazines to list your events at little cost.

TACTIC 71. DIRECT MAIL

Sending a personal letter by mail is one of the quickest promotions to put together and among the fastest ways to get response. A direct mail offer can be a multi-page sales letter, a CD with a handwritten note, a newspaper clipping, a postcard, or even your product catalog.

Studies show direct mail is much more likely to get a response than television, radio, or newspaper advertising.

"Americans spend more than $528 billion annually in response to direct-mail marketing."
~ Houston Business Journal ~

Direct mail is relatively cheap; you can produce exactly the number of letters and envelopes you wish with your home computer. With mail merge, you can personalize each letter by including the person's name and other pertinent details throughout the letter.

Effective direct mail includes an offer that provides a solution to the reader's problem. It invites a call to action; you tell the reader exactly what to do. It must be mailed to a responsive list; if you mail to the wrong list, your offer will mean nothing.

Response rates are affected by your list, your offer, the content in your letter, and the timing. If your list is 20,000 names, test mail to 500 names, measure your response and, if acceptable, then mail to 1,000 more names. If your response rate continues to hold true, mail to 5,000 more names. Always test before rolling out a mail campaign to a larger list.

James got an 8 percent sell-through rate on a client list from an alternative health practitioner by including a personal note of endorsement from her. He sent the same letter (minus the personal endorsement) to subscribers of various health newsletters and magazines. One magazine subscriber list received a 3 percent response, while one of the most popular health newsletter lists brought a dismal 1 percent return. Lesson learned: you can never know for certain what your response rate from any list will be until you test.

Postcards

Postcards are inexpensive to produce in quantity and cheaper to mail than letters. Printed with eye-catching product images, customers have to notice postcards because the card's content is right in their face.

You can test response rates with postcards cheaper and faster than with direct mail letters or CDs. Create print-on-demand postcards and test mail 100 of each offer to different lists. See www.amazingmail.com.

TACTIC 72. CARD DECKS

Card decks include a small package of direct response postcards bundled and mailed to target audiences. There are hundreds of types of card decks aimed at consumers, businesses, and professions. Card decks can target business opportunity seekers, buyers of alternative health services, practitioners, and other specific audiences. Some network marketers have built their entire organizations gathering leads from card decks.

An average card deck may consist of twenty or more 4" by 5½" or larger business reply postcards in a clear plastic wrapping.

Card decks are cheaper than other forms of direct mail. You may pay $18 to $20 per thousand instead of $300 to $500 per thousand letter packages. Companies that produce card decks can handle the graphics and layout, print, and mail the cards, saving you time and money.

Like all paid advertising, you have to test postcard decks to measure the response to your offer. If you get enough leads and new customers to justify the costs, try bigger mailings or try decks going to different audiences.

Design your card deck promotions to be measurable in ways that tell you when you mailed, what your marketing copy was, and who was your target audience. As with all advertising, measure and record your results.

Suppliers of card decks for consumer products:
Leon Henry Inc., www.leonhenryinc.com
Singer Direct, www.singerdirect.com
VentureDirect, www.venturedirect.com
List Services Corp, www.listservices.com
Millard Group, www.millard.com
Suppliers of card decks for network marketing:
www.mlmpostcards.com
www.opportunity-seekers.com
www.wolfenterprises.net/carddecks.html
www.cuttingedgemedia.com

"Shared mail" is related to card decks. This kind of mailing allows you to send your coupons and offers with those of other businesses. You can select specific ZIP or sub-ZIP codes and market areas. For more information on "shared mail" and related types of advertising, see ADVO at www.advo.com/solutions.html and Valpak at www.valpak.com.

TACTIC 73. INSERTS AND RIDE-ALONGS

Every Sunday, your newspaper will carry several inserted promotional pieces from merchants. Have your flyer or article reprint distributed to thousands of recipients by inserting them into newspapers, magazines, or mail order catalogs. Rates can be had from their ad departments.

You can also arrange to have your flyer inserted into the packages being sent to mail order buyers of products like yours. There are hundreds of package insert programs to choose from, including distributors like Hanover House and Fingerhut. You can target your audience by their previous subscriptions and purchases. A big advantage is that if your offer arrives with an order from a well-known brand name catalog, you borrow their credibility. Also, with inserts, you aren't paying anything for postage as the customer has paid shipping for the order.

Prices for inserts range from $40 to $60 per thousand and you must usually order a minimum quantity of several thousand. In general, response rates are typically similar to what you might receive from sending the same offer by mail order, depending on how well you've prepared your promotional piece.

Another form of insert is called statement stuffers. Utilities, credit card companies, magazines, discount clubs, and many other types of businesses send out monthly billing statements to their customers. If your offer can fit on a small 3½" by 6" insert, it will probably be only one of three that postage costs will allow to include as statement stuffers. Delivery is almost guaranteed since these companies have to reach customers whom they invoice. The average price for statement stuffers is around $40 to $50 per thousand, with several thousand as a minimum, depending on the providing service. See above for suppliers of card decks; the same providers often broker inserts as well.

TACTIC 74. DISPLAY ADS

Display ads may be a costly way to market, but ads viewed month after month do instill confidence as readers become familiar with your message. The biggest challenge for the average network marketer is the high cost . Display ads take multiple exposures to get response, which even then, is dependent on the audience, the offer, the timing, and other factors. Many types of publications run display ads including daily newspapers, magazines, college newspapers, church newsletters, and local free publications.

You can tell which ads are working by looking for the ones showing up month after month. Display ads are too costly to run continuously, unless there's response to justify the cost.

Study successful ads and you'll see most of them contain a call to action. They use verbs which compel readers to act.

When designing your own ads, include a persuasive testimonial. It isn't what your ad says about your product that inspires confidence, it's what others with authority say.

Cite marketing statistics that prompt strong feelings that might encourage a sale. Example: "Almost 70 percent of those reaching age 65 will require long-term care at some point in their lives." Scary news, yes?

Sell only one offer per ad and address your words to only one person—your ideal buyer.

You never know who your ad might reach. Maybe you'll attract a potential star ready to shine like one smart sponsor did with Dr. Joe Rubino.

Living Your Dream
by Dr. Joe Rubino

I grew up as what most would consider a poor kid in the inner city of Lawrence, Massachusetts. My dad worked twelve to fourteen hour days for years in the local paper mill to afford the American dream—our family's very own 800-square-foot ranch style home, right across the street from the low income housing projects. Watching families even poorer than us directly across from our front yard gave us the impression of upward mobility and a feeling of gratitude for the modest lifestyle we enjoyed. At about age six, I remember asking my mom if we were poor. I recall her smiling and saying to me, "Joey, we are blessed with abundance. We have a beautiful home. We have plenty of food on the table each night for supper. We love and have each other, have our health, happiness, and our whole lives ahead of us. I wouldn't call that poor, would you?"

My parents helped me attend dental school. After graduating, I hung out my shingle, going into practice with my friend and classmate, Tom Ventullo. Tom and I treated our patients like family and soon we had one of the most successful practices on the North Shore of Massachusetts. Indeed, most would have considered us to be accomplished and successful. But for me, something was missing. I just wasn't sure what it was.

Then, one day I spotted an advertisement in the back of a dental magazine offering the opportunity to supplement, equal, or replace a full time six-figure professional income with an opportunity that offered fulfilling work, time freedom (which I lacked as a dentist mired in the nine-to-five routine) and fun (another missing element in my life). The ad also promised the opportunity for personal development, an attractive concept about which I wished to learn more. As if guided by providence, I learned that the company was holding an introductory meeting on the exact date of our ten-year anniversary in practice. Tom and I saw the serendipity of the occasion and decided to check it out.

We immediately saw the value of creating a residual income asset that would allow us the ability to practice in choice—or not at all—if we so desired. However, there was one small problem. Building a large network would require talking to lots of people. As extreme introverts, this scared the heck out of us. Dentistry was the only thing we could do well and earn a good living at. The trouble was that we were both tired of the routine and largely burned out. We thought there must be a way for us to "reinvent ourselves" to become successful at an entirely new career.

Sure enough, there was. With the help of a few extraordinary coaches (Mike Smith of The Center for Leadership Design, Richard Brooke of High Performance People, and Carol McCall of The World Institute), Tom and I entered into a personal development program that would forever change our lives—and our businesses.

I took on the task of reinventing myself to be the person I *declared* that I would be from that moment forward. I agreed to put aside all the disempowering evidence I had gathered that proved I was a hopeless case.

The result of all of this personal and business development was that I uncovered, often through trial and error, the secrets of success and personal effectiveness, and, with the support of a lot of brilliant people, gained the "key success principles" necessary for any person to be maximally effective with others while growing their business—*with velocity!*

Tom and I applied these "secrets" to our business and launched ourselves to the top of our company, Oxyfresh Worldwide. As I learned what it would take to succeed, I committed to giving those secrets back to others—to support them to become prosperous and live in choice, honoring their most important values and living with no regrets as well.

As a result of my commitment to champion others, I was featured on the cover of the December, 1995 issue of *Success Magazine. The "We Create Millionaires!"* cover story invited readers to learn how successful leaders were creating fortunes at breakneck speed. After all, if an extreme introvert like me could break though self-imposed barriers and become capable of leading others to achieve success, why couldn't anyone?

At the time of my introduction to the concept of personal development, I was both unaware of my most important values of creativity, contribution, inspiration, love, and fun, and certainly not living them. I discovered a particular passion for championing others to reclaim their self-esteem while completing and healing their painful pasts and designing compelling visions for their futures, through the programs offered at www.selfesteemsystem.com.

Joe Rubino is an acclaimed network marketing and personal development trainer, best-selling author of eleven books and audio programs, and CEO of www.CenterForPersonalReinvention.com.

"You must make the product interesting not just make the ad different. And that's what too many of the copywriters in America today don't yet understand."
~ Rooser Reeves ~

Tactic 75. Classified Ads in Print Media

You will find that most magazines and newspapers include a classified ad section. At a much lower cost than for a display ad, you can place text ads in potentially thousands of publications people read every day. The wide availability of classified sections allows great flexibility in focusing on your audiences. They are inexpensive enough that you can test a variety of offers for a small investment.

You can reach readers all around the country through national publications or local residents through regional magazines and newspapers. Since meeting people face-to-face is highly desirable for establishing rapport, consider placing classifieds in nearby daily and community newspapers.

Classified ads don't provide enough space to convince readers to buy product. Typically, classifieds are used as a two-step process. Offer something for free (see the next tactic) and then get readers to visit a website or a phone number for more details.

Classifieds let you zoom in on readers' specific interests. Ads are typically divided into categories like business opportunities, employment, rentals, or items for sale.

How do you know which classified ads work? Simply research a publication's classified section over several issues. As with display ads, the classifieds you see appearing again and again must be pulling responses or the advertiser would not continue to run them.

Here are some tips for writing responsive classifieds:

- Research your target publications first to make sure they reach the audience you wish to sell to.
- Use a brief headline offering a compelling benefit.
- Tell the reader exactly what you choose to have them do.
- Give your phone, website, and/or e-mail contact information.
- Test different categories to see where your ad will perform best.
- Test different lengths of text; if long ads pull better for your offer, run long ads.
- Look at ads appearing continuously for ideas, since those ads are probably getting calls.

For samples of business opportunity ads that get responses, check out USA Today's classifieds over a month's time. Their classified ad rates are relatively costly so the ads showing up day after day are clearly pulling.

TACTIC 76. FREE OFFERS

Ads that offer something for free will get more response then ads that try to sell. Here's a list of offers you can use. Find more ideas in the *Ultimate Guide to Direct Marketing*, by Al Lautensager, available at www.entrepreneurpress.com:

- Free teleseminar
- Free public seminar
- Free meet-and-greet session
- Free special report
- Free CD audio

- Free consultation
- Free product samples
- Free checklist/guide
- Free gift
- Free coupon

Tactic 77. Co-op Ads

In Chapter 9, we gave examples of the leveraging power of partnering with other businesses and professionals. You can also leverage your marketing dollars by partnering with your upline and downline to form cooperative or co-op advertising programs. Co-op advertising refers to creating ad campaigns where the costs and the resulting leads are divided among a group of distributors who all take part in the program. Each participant gets a share of the total leads according to his contribution to the ad cost.

A co-op campaign will entail an investment. Since all advertising costs are at risk, involve an upline leader who has extra funds to get the project started. An upline high-earner can afford the risk, and if there is a loss, claim it as a tax-deductible business expense.

Tactic 78. Your Car As An Ad

You are out there driving your car anyway, so you might as well recoup your expenses. Turn your vehicle into a roaming ad for your business.

Decals can be applied to your car's windows. Vinyl magnetic signs on your doors or side panels can promote your top benefits, phone number, and website.

Your rear window can proclaim a call to action that get's people attention and motivates them to call, like in the following story.

Rear-Window Sign Attracts
Prospects on the Highway
by Charlotte Bacon

I had been in network marketing over a year and was frustrated—I was trying to grow my business but very little seemed to be working. My biggest problem was not having enough leads who were interested.

Buying leads didn't work for me. I tried advertising but never had any success. Then I started using a tool called Sizzle Line® and it made all the difference in the world.

One thing I kept hearing about was to put a sign on the rear window of my car to advertise my business and have people call my Sizzle Line®. So I did. I had a local sign shop create a sign for my rear window. I forget exactly what it said, but after about six weeks with that sign on my car I had a whopping ZERO number of prospects.

I was thinking, "Oh, no. Not again!" I kept hearing about testing different ads to find ones that work best, so I took that sign off and tried a different one. I must not be good at writing ads because that one flopped, too.

In frustration I called the company where I purchased Sizzle Line® and asked for help. They suggested an ad others had success with. It said, "Tired of Living Paycheck to Paycheck? Earn up to thousands extra. For details call xxx-xxx-xxxx."

That made all the difference. Within ten days I had twelve people call and ask for more information. I've since had tons more, but I have to tell you about John.

My husband and I were riding down the Interstate. We were minding our own business when a guy pulled up beside us and began honking his horn. I'm doing 65 mph and I'm thinking, "What in the world is going on?" The guy has his window down and is motioning for me to lower my window. I'm feeling a little concerned, but my husband was next to me so I felt safe enough. I rolled my window down, and this guy, a total stranger, yells over to me and points to the sign on my rear window, "I'm going to call that number in two days!"

I yelled back, "Okay!" and thought, "That was kind of strange." Two days later, he called my Sizzle Line®, got excited and left a message asking to learn more. He said his name was John. I called him back, we set a time to get together, and now he's building a business in our team.

I never would have guessed I could find prospects just by driving down the road . . . but I am.

This story was contributed by GrowthPro, which helps network marketers find their own leads or filter the leads they buy. For more information, visit www.GrowthPro.com/book/

Bumper stickers can attract attention with a headline and web address. It's hard not to read bumper stickers on the car ahead of you when you are waiting for a stop light to change.

Another way to turn your car into a media machine is to exploit the frame that holds your license plates. Companies such as www.autotags4u.com will create a license plate with your custom message for all to see.

Guerrilla Affirmation

I will only advertise to audiences most likely to buy my product or service. I will test all of my direct mail campaigns before investing in more mailings.

Checklist for this Chapter's Tactics

Place a check in the appropriate column for determining how or if you will use a tactic. Then return to your 7-sentence marketing plan - see Chapter 3 - and fill in the appropriate tactics in Step 4 of your plan.

Tactics In This Chapter	Using Well	Using, But Needs Work	Not Using	Not Right At This Time
70. Calendar of Events Listings				
71. Direct Mail				
72. Card Decks				
73. Inserts and Ride Alongs				
74. Display Ads				
75. Classified Ads				
76. Free Offers				
77. Co-op Ads				
78. Your Car As An Ad				

CHAPTER 16

GETTING PEOPLE TO COMMIT

"I am the world's worst salesman, therefore,
I must make it easy for people to buy."
~ F. W. Woolworth ~

You don't have to sell to prosper in network marketing, but you do have to get people to commit. Whether you call it closing, helping, facilitating, sharing, teaching, or any other name, there is a process involved in getting people to buy product and/or sign up as a distributor.

This chapter explores ten ways to influence people to commit to an action by:

1. Getting an immediate result
2. Providing social proof
3. Radiating confidence
4. Educating instead of selling
5. Involving the customer's senses
6. Using three-way calls
7. Being assertive by telling people what to do
8. Giving with generosity
9. Getting on autoship
10. Removing the risk with guarantees.

TACTIC 79. GETTING AN IMMEDIATE RESULT

The pace of life for the average citizen is fast, so in order for you to get someone's attention, your product or opportunity has to produce a measurable result right away. For example, Don's friend Mike was bitten by a brown recluse spider. Even after a trip to the doctor and antibiotic shots, the swelling had not gone down after a couple of days. Don got his friend to try a new product (he had listened to a tape where someone got immediate relief from a similar bite), and within a few hours the swelling subsided. Within 24 hours, the skin around the bite looked normal. Based on that *immediate* life-saving result, Mike signed up and started buying the product regularly.

The same rule of getting a result right away applies to motivating new distributors. Home parties provide a fast way to get cash from sales into a distributor's pockets.

Your goal for all new distributors should be to help them get a check or cash in hand as soon as possible, then teach them how to do the same with their new distributors. A person holds a compensation check in hand, sees the dollar amount, and cannot help but get excited.

The faster you help people experience a result, the easier it will be for them to commit. They basically sell themselves. Another form of quick results is making a great first impression on prospects the way Bonnie Ross Parker advises.

The Quick Connection
by Bonnie Ross-Parker

Deciding to take a stab at network marketing was not an easy decision. Soon after joining a company in November of 2005, I received an announcement that Dr. Charles King, Professor at the University of Illinois in Chicago, was piloting a Certified Network Marketing course. I decided to invest in my decision and take the class. Wow, what an eye opener! It's one thing to take a class; it's another to apply what you learn.

Armed with knowledge and no experience, I set out to "wow" potential customers. It did not go the way I had hoped. I was all over the place spouting the benefits of network marketing and why everyone should have residual income. After exhausting my way through family and friends, I knew I was in trouble.

As with any endeavor, eventually I created my own style, recognizing that being a listener was more effective than getting others to listen to me and, guess what? Results started to come my way. One day, months later, I got asked by someone who had witnessed my success, "What are you doing that is working so effectively?" I answered, "It's as simple as 1 – 2 – 3." It was at that moment I realized what I had been doing and why it worked. The "Quick Connection" was the answer! It was created out of a desperate need to be successful.

Maybe you're a veteran of the networking arena and agree you could be more effective. Or, perhaps you're just getting started and would like to better understand how to network productively. "The Quick Connection" is a reference tool to help you effectively impact others and increase your success.

Here's the familiar scenario: Show up. Shake as many hands as possible. Give out and get as many business cards as you can. Tell everyone, "I'll call you," or expect the people you meet to actually call you. Now, consider another approach that over time will get you better results.

"The Quick Connection" can be implemented any time and in any networking arena. The plan is based on three components: Differentiate, Be Memorable, and Make a Difference. If you focus on attending any business environment with all three or any one of the strategies, your success will increase significantly.

Strategy #1: Differentiate. Being unique distinguishes you from others, especially those that are in the same industry. Remember when you were young and "fitting in" meant doing the same thing as everyone else in the crowd? Being the same was a way of establishing acceptance. In the business world, the opposite is true. You will have an advantage when you differentiate. For example, initiate conversations with people *you don't know.* Ask how he/she got into the industry they are in, what trends they anticipate, or what they did before their current career. Ask what they find to be their biggest challenge. If you're wondering why this line of questioning, it's because most business people are more eager to share what they do than to engage in building rapport with someone else. Find out what a good lead is for the individual you'd like to assist. If you want to get to know another business person, consider extending an invitation to an upcoming networking event as your guest. When you implement strategy #1, the emphasis is off of you and focused elsewhere. This is not typical in networking situations.

Strategy #2: Be Memorable. There are two ways to be memorable—appearance and behavior. In one's appearance consider branding yourself. For example, men can wear unusual ties, different lapel pins, or colors unlike every other man. Women have an easier time. Jewelry can easily help a woman be memorable. Barbara Bush wears her infamous pearls, and Larry King is known for his suspenders. They have branded themselves. I always wear cowboy boots—every day, 365 days a year. While I may not be as well known as Barbara or Larry, having a unique style makes me memorable. People may not remember my name; however, they do remember the lady who always wears cowboy boots. Having a signature style has advantages, especially when you are recognizable.

The second way to be memorable is in your behavior. You must focus on being remembered for the *right* reason—generosity, punctuality, follow-through, integrity, and resourcefulness are examples. Being remembered means leaving positive imprints in everything you say and do. People are watching and will choose to do business with individuals that display consistency and integrity.

Strategy #3: Make A Difference. You never know who you will meet and the difference you can make in someone else's life, or the difference that encounter will make in your life. Replace a simple thank you with "I appreciate you." Go out of your way to make a newcomer feel comfortable at a networking event. Over time, you'll be amazed by how differentiating yourself, being memorable, and making a difference will impact your success. Like anything new, being conscientious and consistent will take time. Let's face it, the marketplace is crowded. Everyone is scurrying for their share of business. Find out for yourself if the effort involved in applying strategies of "The Quick Connection" will be worth the results. Get Up! Get Out! and Get Going!

Bonnie Ross-Parker is the CEO/Founder of The Joy of Connecting—a marketing program serving women nationwide. See www.TheJoyofConnecting.com

Tactic 80. Providing Social Proof

Evidence has shown we tend to follow the crowd, especially when uncertain. We are affected by the actions of those around us; even more often when surrounded by people like us. We even look for what others have done in order to make our own way easier.

Nowhere is social proof more useful as a network marketing tactic than in opportunity meetings and company conventions. Getting people to large meetings allows you to influence a person's decision to commit by making it easier for the person to follow others than to take time worrying about what to do.

In a study treating young children who had a terrible fear of dogs, children simply watched another boy play happily with a dog for twenty minutes a day. After only four days, 67 percent of the children climbed into a playpen with a dog to play with it.

Use social proof in your messages to make it easier for people to decide to act. For instance, "243,665 householders have replaced their old, unhealthy aluminum cookware with our completely safe stainless steel pans. So should you." Include images of people using your product as further proof.

Tactic 81. Radiating Confidence

In network marketing, the only customer you really have to worry about convincing is you. When you're sold on your product and opportunity, you project confidence in your words and your body language.

Studies reveal confidence is the most important factor in the buying decision; more important than quality, price, convenience, and other influences.

Exude trust so others will feel doing business with you is easy, pleasurable, and safe. Studies show how you say your words has five times more impact than the words themselves.

When you meet a prospect for the first time, your projection of confidence will create the first and most important impression of your relationship.

"Inaction breeds doubt and fear. Action breeds confidence and courage. If you want to conquer fear, do not sit home and think about it. Go out and get busy."
~ Dale Carnegie ~

Ways to Build Confidence

For making presentations of any kind, plan ahead of time and practice what you will say. Effective communication is well prepared so that you come across with certainty in both your words and body language.

Prepare for what you would say to a stranger you just met at the mall. Prepare for what you would say to someone who called on the phone for more information. Prepare for what you would say if you were speaking to a group attending an opportunity meeting.

| *Guerrilla Affirmation* | I communicate with people from a genuine desire to help solve their problems. I know that people sense my feelings and appreciate genuineness. |

Practicing your presentations with people you know is a good way to build your confidence level. Get them to ask tough questions to push you into learning more than you'll most likely have time to say under almost any circumstances. Then when you speak to prospects, you will come across as knowledgeable.

Use What Others Say

One of the ways to inspire trust is making it known what others say about your product or opportunity. Use testimonials in your marketing communications.

Mentioning awards will earn you credibility for your products. Be sure to add any product awards to your collection of testimonials and review comments.

Another way to borrow confidence: If your product has been mentioned on TV, include the words "As Seen on TV" on your promotional materials and website pages. Studies have shown it increases response rates.

TACTIC 82. EDUCATING INSTEAD OF SELLING

People are increasingly skeptical of advertising claims and obvious sales pitches. However, it's relatively easy to get someone to download a free educational report, listen to a revealing audio tape, or watch a five-minute presentation that helps them resolve a dilemma, avoid pain in their lives, or save them from losing money.

By educating prospects instead of selling to them, you position yourself as a helpful resource; you provide ways to improve their situation.

Review your marketing plan in Chapter 3 and list the top benefits your product offers to specific audiences. Using these benefits, come up with educational material that solves problems related to your service or product.

Go back to Tactic 11, in Chapter 5. Use the examples there as ideas for how to start building a base of market knowledge. The more authoritative your information, the more respect and trust you'll win from your customers.

"No matter what your product is, you are ultimately in the education business. Your customers need to be constantly educated about the many advantages of doing business with you, trained to use your products more effectively, and taught how to make never-ending improvement in their lives."
~ Robert G Allen ~

Before you can teach, you have to ask your prospects about their challenges, so you will know what education to provide:

• What would your life be like if you had perfect health? (Question for a supplement prospect.)

• How much time could you save if you could book online and get a discount on all your travel? (Question for a travel service prospect.)

• How would it feel to have a legal team working for your business for less than $50 a month? (Question for a legal services prospect.)

Use case studies as educational tools. They help convey your message by demonstrating how your service or product has helped others in similar situations.

TACTIC 83. INVOLVING THE CUSTOMER'S SENSES

Guerrillas increase sales by involving their prospects' five senses. According to Gilmore and Pine, advisors to Fortune 500 companies, "The best way to market any offering (goods, service, or experience) is with an experience so engaging that potential customers can't help but pay attention and pay up."

"Touch your customer, and you're halfway there."
~ Estee Lauder ~

When making a presentation, exhibiting at an event, or just talking to someone over coffee, come prepared to engage one or more of the senses with your product or offer. If your product line is edible, have samples of the best-tasting items. Make great tasting recipes using ingredients from your line. Essential oils can be smelled and applied to the skin. Use sound and sight with a DVD presentation.

Retail businesses are using smells to affect shopper's moods. It's one of the top 10 trends to watch in 2007, according to Advertising Age. "People will make quicker decisions, be willing to pay more, and most likely be so emotionally engaged that they are removed from the rational part of their behavior," says Martin Lindstrom, author of the book, *Brand Sense*.

TACTIC 84. USING THREE-WAY CALLS

A three-way call is a phone conference between three people. Most U.S. phone service providers allow you this option on a pay-per-call billing or unlimited three-way calls as a monthly service option. Setting up a three-way call is easy. Start by dialing the first party you wish

> *Guerrilla*
> *Affirmation*
>
> I focus on getting an immediate *measurable result* from customers who use my products and distributors who are growing their business.

to speak to. While you have that person on the line, tell the person you are going to put him on hold and then briefly push the receiver button down. You'll hear a soft tone indicating you can now dial a second number. When the third party comes on, hold the receiver button down briefly then release it again to bring in the first party.

After you have begun a relationship with a prospect and they are considering joining your company, introduce them to your upline with a three-way call. First, set up an appointment for the call with your prospect and your upline member. Once you're on the phone to your prospect or your upline, you use three-way calling to bring in the other party. Introduce your upline, then let him or her present while you listen and take notes. After you've done several three-ways with your upline and become familiar with how to talk to new prospects, encourage your downline to use you for their three-way calls.

Tactic 85. Being Assertive: Tell People What To Do

Most prospects will not do what you choose for them to do unless you tell them to do it. You have to spell it out for them and make it clear what action they must take. You can do this verbally when making presentations and you can do this in your ads and promotional material.

*"If you are not moving closer to what you
want in sales (or in life), you probably
aren't doing enough asking."*
~ Jack Canfield ~

There are many ways to ask for the sale without sounding like a car salesman. Examples are:

- Can I write this up for you?
- Will you be putting this on your charge card?
- How would you like to pay for this?
- I think you'll be pleased. Let me take your order for this today.
- As soon as you sign the application, we can get started helping you build your business right away.
- Based on what you've just learned, are you ready to get started?
- Let's take care of the paperwork now so you can get started right away.
- Is Wednesday or Thursday the best day to deliver your order?
- The company can ship your product order right away, if you will just sign the application form right here.

Expect the sale

Part of asking for the sale is expecting it to happen. Richard Brooke, president of Oxyfresh, says you don't get what you want in life, you get what you expect.

If you expect to fail, you will. If you expect to win, you will. One immediate way to change your results is to change how you use language. Instead of saying "I want to be a Diamond distributor," use the words, "I choose to be a Diamond distributor" or "I am a Diamond distributor." Choose to expect that people will buy your products and more of them will.

Tactic 86. Giving with Generosity

It is a deeply held social obligation to reciprocate when given a gift, according to Robert Cialdini, PhD and author of *Influence: The Psychology of Persuasion.* Numerous studies have shown that we automatically attempt to repay what someone else has provided. Before you ask someone to commit, give that person something first.

Amway employed this "law" in a program that brought measurable results. The company created a kit of samples of their various household products— detergent, shampoo, cleansers, etc. Distributors could leave the sample kit with prospects and tell them to use the samples as they liked for a couple of days at no cost. When the trial period was over, the distributor would return to the prospect, collect the kit, and take orders for product. The distributor could then refill the sample bottles and start over with another lead. Happy distributors reported the program resulted in the biggest increase in sales they experienced from any other kind of marketing they had tried.

Helping Instead of Selling
Mary Billeter Young

In September of 1985, I was at the Utah State Fair talking to a gentleman in a booth about aluminum welding rod. In the middle of the conversation, he put a little bottle of a natural sweetener in my face and asked me if I was interested in health. I said that I might be, and with that began my introduction to network marketing.

He invited me to a meeting that introduced his products. I became very excited and wanted to tell all my family members and friends about this new discovery. I had just returned from South America where I had been trying to recover some losses from an investment in a gold mining adventure that had become a financially devastating experience for my family and many other people.

Mercury poisoning from the gold recovery process had left me in ill health. In addition, the financial hardship of the failed investment made our lives very difficult, eventually causing my father's death.

My father had been a chiropractor. We had grown up in a health-minded home, so I was naturally excited about the health possibilities of the new products. However, I knew nothing about the MLM world and believed that those at the top sucked the money from those at the bottom. Since I was at the bottom, I didn't like that. But I decided I would just ignore the business and help people get healthier. I energetically made my presentations and signed up everyone I could sit down with at the kitchen table. Because of my own enthusiasm, people became excited. It was very exhilarating in the beginning.

My first commission check was only $5, which did put a question in my mind. By the third month, my check had reached $500, and when it went over $1,000, I thought I had become rich. People started asking me about the business and I couldn't tell them anything. So one night I decided I had better take a look at the marketing plan. I was amazed at how simple it was, and how easy it was to make money from. I started analyzing my organization and determined how best to work it.

At the time, I was driving a 1968 red VW that had no heat and wouldn't go in reverse. So I had to be very careful where I parked. I would park far away from the hotel entrance when I went to meetings so no one would see that I had to wear a blanket around my shoulders during the winter. I determined that if I structured my organization right, I could qualify for a car. After one year in the business, I bought a 300D Mercedes with a commission check of around $10,000.

I could hardly believe it was happening. Actually, I was afraid to get the Mercedes, but a friend assured me it would retain its resale value better than another model, so I determined that if I couldn't pay for it, I would just sell it. I financed it for seven years and paid it off in two years with the car bonus money from the company.

Within two years, I paid off all the debt for my whole family. That was a glorious moment for us and my heart still fills with joy when I think of those times. My philosophy was to help everyone become successful.

It made no difference to me where people were in my downline, because even if they weren't in my payout, they were in the payout of others in my organization that would benefit and perhaps get more excited about the business. I loved everyone and thrilled at their success. I watched many people who didn't think they could stand up and speak to others develop into leaders and build tremendous organizations of their own. I built a very powerful organization that didn't need me. I taught them to look into their organizations to see who they could help. Eventually, they didn't look up to me. When we met again at events and conventions, we had a grand reunion sharing in everyone's growth and success.

Looking back with gratitude, those first ten years in network marketing taught me the ropes of the business from the distributor side, preparing me for the role that I carry now. Alongside my husband and company founder Gary Young, we have grown Young Living Essential Oils from a little struggling nothing-to-pay-attention-to company to a world-class producer of natural products for the health and well-being of mankind.

Mary Young is a successful veteran network marketer and serves as Executive Vice President at Young Living in Lehi, Utah. See www.youngliving.us

Tactic 87. Getting on Autoship

Autoship allows customers to receive pre-scheduled shipments of selected products every month, charged to their credit cards. If your company offers autoship, get on the program yourself. Distributors tend to do what you do so getting on autoship is a training tool.

When you sign up a new member, explain how commissions are paid on sales volumes and the surest way to guarantee getting a check is to get everyone on the autoship program. With autoship, you are guaranteed that you and your team will qualify for personal volume (PV) every month.

TACTIC 88. REMOVING THE RISK WITH GUARANTEES

Offering a money-back guarantee removes risk from the buyer's mind. It's vital to provide this assurance when people are unfamiliar with you and your company. Since most companies provide some form of guarantee, state the company's policy up front.

When communicating with prospects, consider adding another level of reassurance by backing up the company's guarantee with one of your own.

Prospects looking at your product or opportunity think, "What's this going to cost me?" When you can confidently say "It won't cost you anything if you don't find it does everything we say it will," you've removed the gamble behind trying something new.

"Sales people should take lessons from their kids. What does the word 'no' mean to a child? Almost nothing."
~ Jim Rohn ~

Checklist for this Chapter's Tactics

Place a check in the appropriate column for determining how or if you will use a tactic. Then return to your 7-sentence marketing plan - see Chapter 3 - and fill in the appropriate tactics in Step 4 of your plan.				
Tactics In This Chapter	Using Well	Using, But Needs Work	Not Using	Not Right At This Time
79. Getting an Immediate Result				
80. Providing Social Proof				
81. Radiating Confidence				
82. Educating Instead of Selling				
83. Involving the Customer's Senses				
84. Using Three-Way Calls				
85. Being Assertive: Tell People What to Do				
86. Giving with Generosity				
87. Getting on Autoship				
88. Removing the Risk with Guarantees				

CHAPTER 17

TACTICS TO HELP YOU FOLLOW UP

"Some people fold after making one timid request. They quit too soon. Keep asking until you find the answers. In sales there are usually four or five no's before you get a yes."
~ Jack Canfield ~

Follow-up fosters ongoing relationships. It's smart marketing because statistics indicate that, by retaining just 5 percent more customers, you can increase your compensation from 25 to 125 percent.

One survey revealed that customers stop buying not because they are unhappy, but simply because they feel unappreciated and ignored.

Earning people's trust takes time. Follow-up makes you familiar. If a customer chooses to do business with you, it's because, on some level, you've earned that individual's confidence.

In measured and appropriate doses, familiarity turns into credence. Guerrilla follow-up strategies transform product buyers into loyal customers and then into advocates—people who will trumpet your product's praises and refer more customers to you.

Remember, most people are busy with their day-to-day issues. Your marketing communication may attract their attention one day and be forgotten soon after, because the person's priorities shift to deal with what's going on in the present moment. Without regular follow-up, the more time that lapses after your initial contact, the less important your message becomes.

This chapter helps you stay in your customer's thoughts through the use of these guerrilla tactics:
- A follow-up calendar
- A customer reactivation letter
- Newsletters
- Conference calls

TACTIC 89. FOLLOW-UP CALENDAR

Make follow-up easy by building in a system for future contact with every prospect. With a system in place, you won't forget to communicate regularly and your people won't feel ignored. Use a contact management system as described in Chapter 8. When you are gathering your prospect's phone, e-mail, and address, learn and record how people prefer to communicate. Schedule five follow-ups to different people a day, five days every week. That's 1,300 contacts per year, many of whom will buy more product or refer more business to you.

When you say you are going to follow through with someone, be sure you do. The fastest way to lose trust is to neglect doing what you say you will.

Excuses to Stay in Touch

For times when you can't think of a good reason to reconnect with your contacts or you feel resistant to the effort, here are more than sixty excuses for reminding people of you. Many of the reasons for following up provide opportunities to get to know your customers better. When you know about your prospects, you can tailor future follow-ups to:

√Provide something they will perceive as beneficial and valuable—such as a discount coupon or a research study;

√Show you care (because you made extra effort to address issues relevant to their interests);

√Make each prospect feel important, not forsaken.

Follow-Up with Prospects To:

- Make an appointment to meet again
- Thank someone after meeting with you
- Drop by in person after a meeting just to say hello
- Seek a sponsor for a home party or meeting
- Invite someone to a home party or meeting
- Confirm an upcoming meeting or home party with a phone call or e-mail
- Thank someone for sponsoring a home party or meeting
- Send a product brochure which answers a special concern
- Send a catalog
- Send a CD, DVD or video
- Send a product sample
- Send testimonials from satisfied customers
- Learn if a prospect received your letter, flyer, or communication
- Thank someone for their time even if they didn't buy

Follow-Up With Customers To:

- Say "thank you" after a sale
- Announce a new product release
- Announce a product on sale or at a discount
- Check to see if a customer got their order
- Learn if the customer is happy with their product
- Send an FAQ sheet (Frequently Asked Questions about products, along with answers)
- Send educational articles that explain the benefits and details of products

• Send a series of autoresponders with helpful tips
• Keep track of a customer's progress using a new product
• Advise about discontinued products
• Send a newsletter with product information
• Ask for referrals from happy customers
• Thank someone for a referral
• Let a referring person know that his referral bought product, experienced a result, or became active in the business
• Inform customers of other products in your catalog they aren't currently using
• Ask for feedback on how well you did for service and quality of product
• Make your customer a personal offer because he or she has purchased before
• Suggest gift ideas for holidays and special occasions

Follow-Up With Distributors To:

• Welcome a new member to your organization
• Send a monthly newsletter with tips and news
• Send testimonials from distributors who are achieving financial freedom
• Send a postcard or flyer with a schedule of training events
• Check progress on distributors who have shared their goals
• Send an FAQ sheet about network marketing
• Send a CD, DVD or video explaining the compensation plan or bonus incentives
• Announce an improvement to the comp plan
• Announce a contest
• Congratulate someone in your downline after they make a sale or reach the next level in the comp plan

- Congratulate someone on a promotion or an accomplishment, even if unrelated to your MLM
- Express your pleasure in working with someone
- Invite a distributor to dinner out as a way of expressing appreciation
- Invite a distributor to play golf or tennis, or go hiking or sailing to catch up or discuss potential strategies
- Let people know when you are teaching a class in their area or at a national event
- Ask for feedback on a presentation
- Offer to link to a distributor's website from your own
- Send a news clipping or copy of an article relating to your company's products or industry
- Thank someone for taking the time to attend an event or presentation.
- Offer a marketing course to your team members
- Check to see if someone did something they agreed to do in a previous communication or meeting

Miscellaneous Reasons to Follow-Up:

- Announce any news
- Thank someone for doing you a favor
- Take a survey
- Share an idea
- Offer to buy a cup of coffee or tea
- Send a gift
- Handle a problem the customer or distributor had with the company or product
- Make up for a mistake on your part
- Wish a happy birthday
- Acknowledge an anniversary
- Celebrate holidays other than Christmas, including Thanksgiving, Mother's Day, or

Valentine's Day
- Wish someone a speedy recovery
- Congratulate someone on having anything new (a marriage, baby, car, boat, or home)
- Offer condolences for a loss

Ways to Connect

There's nothing like one-on-one meetings for earning trust and building confidence. Face-to-face interactions account for 73 percent of sales, according to the Direct Selling Association.

For those times you can't be there in person, technology has improved the variety of ways we can communicate with others and build relationships. Multiply all the above excuses for follow-up by the number of ways you can contact someone, and you have an arsenal of hundreds of potential follow-up messages. Here are seven ways of contacting people:

1. Face-to-face
2. Telephone
3. Postal mail
4. Fax
5. E-mail
6. Instant messaging
7. Web cam live video

Don't make a secret of your availability. Let it be known when callers can expect you to return calls or when you're in town. Fast response to calls and e-mails earns people's attention. Delaying your response will trigger abandonment issues.

"Spend a lot of time talking to customers face to face. You'd be amazed how many companies don't listen to their customers."
~ Ross Perot ~

TACTIC 90. CUSTOMER REACTIVATION LETTER

According to one study, the average business loses about 20 percent of its customers annually. Over half of all businesses consider lapsed customers as forfeited business and do little or nothing to get them back. However, many of these former customers can be reactivated.

Statistically, the average company has a 20 to 40 percent probability of getting lapsed customers to buy again. Compare that to the only 5 to 20 percent probability of making a first sale to a new prospect and you'll see the payoff in marketing to customers who've already proven they will buy your product.

Go through your geneology and list the names of people who haven't ordered in a couple of months. Create a mail-merge document which will become a personalized customer reactivation letter. In your letter, convey that you miss the person as a customer and you would like to have them back.

Here are some tips to include in your letter to help reactivate former customers:

•Learn which products customers bought previously, so you can point out the benefits of reordering.

•Include testimonials from satisfied customers in your letter.

•Include a sample of another product that's getting great customer feedback.

•If there's a special promotion going on, emphasize the urgency to order now to save money.

•State a reason why you are writing. For instance, you are updating your records and would like to make sure the person knows he qualifies for a discount, or is about to lose the ability to order wholesale.

•Add a photo of yourself. Customers like to know (or be reminded of) whom they are doing business with.

Consider sending lapsed customers a rebate certificate if they buy by the end of the month. If your company doesn't provide rebate or gift certificates, make up your own.

MLM companies who use customer reactivation incentive offers to members who've dropped off the active list have achieved great results. If your company doesn't have a reactivation program, get back some of your hard-earned business by starting your own.

Tactic 91. Newsletters

As a follow-up tool, a newsletter positions you as a source of support through delivering helpful hints and news to subscribers on a consistent basis.

Roger C. Parker of www.onepagenewsletters.com advises preparing an attractive, easy-to-read, monthly, one-topic, educationally oriented, one-page newsletter to distribute from your website or as an e-mail attachment. Your newsletter enables you to:

•Remain constantly visible to your customers and interested prospects;

•Lower the high costs associated with conventional marketing;

•Pre-sell your competence and differentiate yourself from your competition while adding to a reservoir of information your subscribers can use over and over again.

It costs an average of six times more to accumulate a new customer than to sell to a customer who knows you. A newsletter can help you sell more products to past customers and help keep distributors active longer.

Make your newsletter content beneficial or people will not subscribe. There's plenty of room in your newsletter to include your own ads and announcements while presenting valuable material readers are hungry to receive.

Create graphically attractive newsletters that convey your professionalism. Well-designed publications add to your authority as a resource.

Tactic 92. Conference Calls

Conference calls infuse your team with energy and motivation. Calls help everyone get on the same page about developments and opportunities with training, products, and compensation bonuses. Calls provide the opportunity for repeated contact through weekly or monthly gatherings by phone.

"He will win whose army is animated by the same spirit throughout all its ranks."
~ Sun Tzu, Art of War ~

Calls allow the best ideas to be shared, so that everyone who participates feels part of the team, and newer distributors get to learn proven approaches. In addition to an ongoing follow-up tactic, distributors can use conference calls as a recruiting tool.

Because conference calls are scheduled, they can help build confidence through assuring callers of a regular event. If your upline doesn't have a call setup, consider starting your own with a service like www.freeconference.com.

Making Follow-Up More Effective

According to a study conducted by the Association of Sales Executives, 81 percent of all sales happen on or after the fifth contact. When follow-up is incorporated as a scheduled tactic, you automatically introduce repetition of your message into your marketing campaign.

| *Guerrilla Affirmation* | I *follow-up* quickly and consistently with leads, prospects, customers, and distributors. I schedule follow-up at regular intervals. |

Here are several ways to generate better returns from your follow-up and how to use follow-up approaches that strengthen your relationships:

• Express a reason why you are following up and your results will improve. A Harvard study showed that when asking someone to do something for you, you will get more compliance when you express the reason and use the word "because." For example, if you are calling opportunity seeker leads purchased from a service, you might say that you are calling back *because* they filled in a form requesting more information on starting a home business.

• In follow-up communications, focus your intention on solving problems rather than getting sales. Do this and people will look forward to your contact instead of asking you to leave them alone.

• When following up, keep your communications warm and personalized. Mass mailings that do not address individuals by name fail to engage. Using first names in e-mail subject lines has been found to more than double response rates.

• Handwritten notes generate warmth and connection. Try sending a handwritten thank-you note to customers after their first sale.

• Each time you make a follow-up contact is an opportunity to learn more about your customer; important family members, upcoming special events, work- and play- related information. As mentioned earlier, take notes when you're talking so you can jot down points to remember when making future contacts.

• Each time you follow-up, refer to something spoken of in a previous contact. Even if someone doesn't remember all the details, your linking to a previous communication makes you more familiar to them.

• After revisiting a point made last time, bring up a new benefit or added value to the person. For example, you could say, "Did I mention that _____ (your product name) also helps prevent colds?"

• Without permission from prospects, future follow-ups will most likely be perceived as an annoyance. To prevent this, tell prospects in your first communication with them that you would like to talk more later, and learn at that time if they are agreeable to hearing from you again. By giving you this permission, they will have automatically qualified themselves as a candidate for follow-up communications.

"Often people attempt to live their lives backwards; they try to have more things, or more money, in order to do more of what they want, so they will be happier. The way it actually works is the reverse. You must first be who you really are, then do what you need to do, in order to have what you want."
~ Margaret Young ~

Checklist for this Chapter's Tactics

Place a check in the appropriate column for determining how or if you will use a tactic. Then return to your 7-sentence marketing plan - see Chapter 3 - and fill in the appropriate tactics in Step 4 of your plan.				
Tactics In This Chapter	Using Well	Using, But Needs Work	Not Using	Not Right At This Time
89. Follow-Up Calendar				
90. Customer Reactivation Letter				
91. Newsletters				
92. Conference Calls				

Guerrilla Affirmation

I actively seek ways to *amaze* customers and team members with outstanding personalized service. I follow up to handle all complaints promptly.

CHAPTER 18

DUPLICATION

According to census surveys, the failure rate for most start-up businesses is 50 to 80 percent in their first year. The failure rate for start-up franchises, however, is less than 10 percent, as reported in the *Wall Street Journal.*

Why the big difference?

Franchises come with a complete system and set of procedures for how to run the business, step-by-step, addressing any situation the new owner might face. Most franchise training systems take the new owner by the hand, and lead him to profitability, day after day. The owner doesn't waste time reinventing the wheel. However, the average non-franchise business is typically started by someone with technical skills, but little or no training in running a business.

Do you provide distributors a system in your network marketing business? Are you teaching others to use the system and to teach their people?

This chapter will show you how to create, organize, and implement procedures anyone can follow to succeed with your opportunity. It's what duplication is all about.

Success in network marketing comes from duplication. Telling someone to be duplicable is easy; achieving it is a different story. That's because:

1. People are not alike.

2. Not all people are motivated by the same goals.

3. Some people won't take the same actions regardless of the incentives.

4. Initial fever has gone cold.

5. Some people are naturally rebellious.

6. Some people dislike being told what they have to do.

7. Some people were only pretending interest when they signed up.

There's not much you can do about the last three types. The best policy is to be polite to them, but don't waste time trying to get them on board.

The first four kinds of people are more likely to respond to the system in this book because it:

• Provides a multitude of tactics that will appeal to and work for different personality types;

• Allows people to align their marketing plan with their specific goals;

• Customizes an individual's action steps to fit his or her lifestyle;

• Provides excitement through results.

TACTIC 93. USING A SYSTEM

Systems are sets of procedures to follow for advancing your business under any given circumstances you encounter. You'll find the high-earners in your upline use some kind of system to organize their daily activities and to train distributors.

*"Your needs will be met once you can
find a way of projecting energy and
fulfilling someone else's need."*
~ Stuart Wilde ~

If you don't have an upline with a system, create your own "Standard Operating Procedures" or SOP manual with simple instructions for:

- Showing customers how to order products
- Orienting distributors on how to get started
- Creating a marketing plan
- Creating a marketing calendar
- Creating a calendar for following up
- How to sponsor a home party
- How to display products at a public event
- Scripts for what to say when talking to leads
- Setting up opportunity meetings
- Creating training events.

Many of the above sets of procedures will already be available to you from your upline or company. If not, use the chapters in this book as guidelines to create your own. *Guerrilla Multilevel Marketing* isn't just a book— it's training system you can pass on.

Creating procedures for every aspect of your network marketing business clarifies all the necessary steps. A system makes you completely confident, so that, when talking to prospective business builders, you can speak about your opportunity with ease and conviction.

You can develop a system using life experiences. Janine Avila's network marketing system arose from the necessity of raising a house full of kids.

The Secret is in the System
by Janine Avila

As a young girl growing up, I had always wanted to have a large family. I wanted to be a great mom. I pictured myself at home, baking cookies as I awaited the school bus, anticipating my children's arrival so I could hear about their day, offering my advice and just being there
... I didn't want to miss it. Then life tossed me a curve and I found myself a single mom. I was at a loss. Where do you go when you have five kids to care for, a mortgage to pay, and no time? Network marketing, that's where. I had found my solution.

Although I started out as a distributor just to get a discount on my product, I began to realize the possibility of being able to have it all. I had developed systems to manage my large family. I had to—otherwise it was chaos. Initially I didn't think I had the skills to run a successful business, but I soon learned that the systems I had created at home to manage my large family were also powerful in business. When I incorporated those systems into my business, I saw dramatic results. As an added benefit, I found the new skills I was learning in business could be applied to my life at home. For example, we began to have "Family Council Meetings" complete with pre-printed agendas. The kids got handbooks with the guidelines and everyone had their own "inbox." It was fun and it worked

I planned my days; everything was on paper and organized. I made sure I got to games, appointments, and meetings by creating a system that held the kids accountable for tracking family events and their own time. This empowered them and freed up my time.

I found that in my network marketing business the same principles applied. I showed people how to plan and get organized; I trained them well and they in turn prospered. It was easier to train well and watch the personal growth that occurred than it was to do it all for them. As my business grew, I continued to use creativity and great mentors to adjust my systems. We made it work. I use color-coded time slots to block time for business, personal, and family in my planner. I never leave home without it.

When I trained my distributors to follow a simple system, my business skyrocketed.

My income went up, I had more time at home, and I felt great about the example I was setting. I love bringing people into the industry to show them a way that they, too, can have it all . . . *if t*hey follow the "system."

Several years after I began my new career in network marketing, I was able to adopt two teenage boys who were in a foster home. I was now the proud mother of seven. This was made possible because I had the income, the time, and the confidence. I soared to number one in the nation in recruiting and promoting. My dream to be a great mom was a reality, I was not only able to schedule the time I needed when my kids were home, but I was able to drive them on field trips in a nice car. We didn't just survive, we thrived. My organizing methods enabled us to step up to a new level at home and I found that raising seven children was not a burden, it was a blessing.

Since that time I have traveled across the U.S., Canada, and even Russia to teach the principles of network marketing and the secrets to my success system. My passion for this industry gave me the life I wanted.

My children have all grown and left home now. My baby, who was two when I started, is 26 now, and I have 13 grandkids. Life is good, and I was there when they were there. I have a philosophy that it's not what happens to you in life, but how you respond to it. I keep a sense of humor and love to learn new ideas that I can share with others. To live a life of no regrets . . . now *that's* freedom.

Today Janine Avila is a motivational speaker, network marketing trainer and coach. She continues to build a successful network marketing business with long-time business associate and mentor Richard Brooke at Oxyfresh. You can visit her website at www.janineavila.com.

Place your procedures in a loose-leaf binder with dividers separating the different topics; this is your SOP for your network marketing business. Make extra copies of frequently asked for procedures. When a new distributor signs up, give them a handout telling them what to do and then go over the steps with them.

Here's an example of a procedure to follow for what to say to brand new distributors:

1. "We have an orientation call next _____."
2. "You will learn how to get started in the business and it will take only about an hour of your time."
3. "Nearly all of your questions and concerns will be addressed at this orientation."
4. "Can I get your commitment to be on the call so you will know what steps to take to maximize your results from this business?"

Create similar sets of steps to take, questions to ask, and procedures for all the circumstances you and your distributors can imagine for how to grow your network marketing businesses.

"One of the things that may get in the way of people being lifelong learners is that they're not in touch with their passion. If you're passionate about what it is you do, then you're going to be looking for everything you can to get better at it."
~ Jack Canfield ~

Become Likeable

People in your group will follow your lead, but only if they like you. If you would have duplication in your organization, become lovable. Here are some lovable characteristics to adopt:

- Be a friend first, a sponsor second
- Listen more than you talk
- Acknowledge instead of criticize
- Admit your mistakes
- Be prompt in returning messages
- Be fast in getting problems resolved
- Be trustworthy
- Be totally present with whom you're speaking. Almost every person has an under-fulfilled longing for genuine, undistracted, one-on-one personal attention.

Offer More Choices

Guerrilla Multilevel Marketing offers 100 tactics so people can build a successful network marketing business in a way that suits their individual personality.

Most of your new recruits don't have a marketing or business background, but they do have characteristics that let you know how best to help them. For example, is your new distributor shy or a real networker? Does he or she know how to use the Internet, or even desire to? Can this person talk to a group of people, or is the very notion of public speaking upsetting?

Shy people may actually compensate by going online more often. They may know more about websites and search engines than they do about talking to others. Does your system allow for helping someone with this kind of personality? Can you support shy people to discover and work from where they are strong, instead of pushing them into stress and precipitating their dropping out of the program?

This is not to say some people can't use or even appreciate a little push to grow personally. But shoving everyone in the same direction, as if they were all cast from the same mold, is a sure recipe for attrition. Offer more choices and people will stay involved longer, which means bigger checks for them and for you.

Checklist for this Chapter's Tactics

Place a check in the appropriate column for determining how or if you will use a tactic. Then return to your 7-sentence marketing plan - see Chapter 3 - and fill in the appropriate tactics in Step 4 of your plan.				
Tactics In This Chapter	Using Well	Using, But Needs Work	Not Using	Not Right At This Time
93. Using a System				

CHAPTER 19

IMPROVING YOUR RESULTS

"Success leaves clues."
~ Tony Robbins ~

Our business stops growing when we stop growing. From time to time, every network marketer hungers for an infusion of new ideas and strategy. This chapter provides ways to help you boost your results through:

• Providing outrageously good customer service
• Becoming accountable
• Associating with successful people
• Joining or forming a Master Mind group
• Continuing education
• Capitalizing on your compensation plan
• Tracking and measuring your results
• Persisting with your promotions

TACTIC 94. PROVIDING OUTRAGEOUSLY GOOD CUSTOMER SERVICE

An excellent strategy for inspiring customers to start talking to their friends is to go beyond your customer's expectations of service. When new customers place their first order, find out the delivery date from the company. Call the evening of that day and ask if they received what they ordered. If there is a concern or complaint, listen carefully and get the issue resolved without delay. Answer all questions and offer further support with user tip sheets or research studies that assure each customer that they made the right choice.

Your network marketing parent company provides customer service to free you to do what you do best, which is building relationships and bringing in new customers. You can win over your customers and distributors even more by adding your own personal touch of service by remembering:

- 68 percent of customers stop doing business with a company when they get poor service;
- It costs 5 times as much to get a new customer as it does to keep an existing one;
- Customers who are mistreated tell 10 to 20 other people about their problem;
- Satisfied customers do more than buy again—on average, they tell 5 others of their experience.

"This may seem simple, but you need to give customers what they want, not what you think they want. And, if you do this, people will keep coming back."
~ John Ilhan ~

People like people who help them. Here are several simple ways to shine in the eyes of your buyers and distributors:

- Respond to messages; people like people who make time for them.
- Respond quickly. According to the most recent studies, people prize their time greatly; they desire that their phone calls be handled fast; their orders processed immediately; and their complaints handled now.
- Be a sponsor who collaborates, not competes.

• Continually acknowledge those you sponsor; people love to be recognized.

• Answer your own phone as often as possible. One survey showed that 74 percent of callers were unlikely to order from a recording.

• Be friendly; avoid talking to people when you're feeling down.

Studies show that people who are nice are healthier, have fewer divorces and make more money, according to authors, Linda Kaplan Thaler and Robin Koval in their book, "The Power of Nice: How to Conquer the Business World With Kindness."

• Agree immediately; people like others who understand how they feel.

• Follow up on complaint issues.

• Avoid arguing.

• Accept responsibility for misunderstandings even when it isn't your fault. Simply say it was your mistake of miscommunication and ask how you can fix the issue.

• Follow up with the company customer service to make certain a problem has been fixed; then let your customer know the results.

• Don't over-promise and then fail to deliver. Always be honest about what you can get done and, when possible, over-deliver.

• If your company offers a risk-free guarantee, let your customers know about it.

• Keep your promises; people like those they can rely on.

• When your distributors have problems with the company, learn what you can do to make things right.

Tactic 95. Becoming Accountable

Identify those in your upline who are actively building and get on their team. Being accountable to a coach or mentor once a week helps you focus. Studies have shown that people are more likely to take action when they are part of a team.

When you work alone, it's easy to neglect the actions that will take you forward in your business. Having someone to whom you are accountable can make all the difference. Partner with an upline who will agree to give you homework assignments week to week. Before the next week's due date, you take the actions to achieve the goal you agreed to meet. When you become accountable to someone else, you are more likely to take action.

Tactic 96. Associating with Successful People

If you ask ten different MLM leaders how they built their business, you will probably hear ten different approaches. But most of them will agree that investing time with successful, positive-thinking people has made all the difference.

There is scientific evidence to support the claim that you become like the people you associate with. Neuroscientists have discovered something in our brains called "mirror neurons." These neurons play a role in our survival as a species. We learn from observing and imitating others. You can easily observe behavior mirroring in high school kids who copy each other's dress, hair, and speech.

However, mirror neurons cause us to imitate others even without our conscious intention. If you hang out with people who are constantly complaining, you'll find yourself doing the same. If you associate with people who consistently self-sabotage themselves, you will find yourself nonconsciously mimicking their behavior.

---

*"You are a product of your environment.
So choose the environment that will best
develop you toward your objective. Analyze
your life in terms of its environment. Are the
things around you helping you toward success
- or are they holding you back."*
~ Clement Stone ~

Another phenomenon backed up by scientific research, discussed in a Cambridge University Press book, is known as "emotional contagion." This is a powerful influencer that should make you consider carefully with whom you spend time around.

"When we are talking to someone who is depressed, it may make us feel depressed, whereas if we talk to someone who is feeling self-confident and buoyant, we are likely to feel good about ourselves," say the authors.

Direct selling companies have incorporated the positive use of emotional contagion into their culture. As reported in a study by the Yale School of Management, the Mary Kay Cosmetics company has transferred enthusiasm through the use of songs, recognition dinners, and national meetings where positive emotions were intentionally spread. Amway has also used emotional contagion, calling it "positive programming." According to the Yale study, Amway constantly encourages its members to stay positive and to transfer that positivity to others.

Homeless to Millionaire in Two Years
by Dani Johnson

Growing up in a drug inflicted and abusive home, I had no dreams, no goals, no confidence, and no self-esteem. I was first exposed to direct sales at the age of nineteen. I didn't think someone like me could ever succeed in anything. So the excuse and objection that I gave my sponsor was, "This is great for you, but not for me. I'm sure you will do awesome at this, but there is no way I could do this business."

My sponsor persisted anyway. He put me in front of conference calls and brought me to an eight-hour training. During that training, I heard a testimony from a man who spent twenty-five years in the corporate world as an engineer only to be laid off. His words echoed in my ears: "Don't make the same mistake I did of building equity in someone else's company . . . only to lose it all in one day. Get in direct sales now. Don't waste twenty-five years like I did. I now make more monthly than I used to all year long!" That hit me hard. I figured, even if I totally mess this up by 90 percent . . . I would still be doing better than if I work for someone else, even if it took me twenty years to get where he is. So I quit my job and came in full time.

The next six months I failed miserably, and I mean miserably. I couldn't sponsor anyone or sell a thing. Then I met someone who was making $15,000 a month—which was $15,000 more than I was making. We had both started the very same month, yet it was obvious that I was doing something wrong. I begged him to teach me how to crawl, walk, and then run. He agreed to work with me, but only if I attended a millionaire's two-day training seminar in another state. Not willing to entertain the thought of failure, I found a way and made it happen and thank God for that. I came out of that first seminar and brought in twenty-five business builders in eight days and earned $4,000. That was more than all six months combined. Something massively changed for me in two days at that seminar. The next check was $11,000, then $15,000, then $21,000.

This sudden rise to success brought recognition from top leaders and executives in the company. Success also attracted the attention of the so-called "man of my dreams" who promised me the world and swept me off my feet. I wound up in huge trouble. My husband took off with everything and left me with a $35,000 debt and $2.03 cents to my name. I went from being on the top of the world to the bottomless pit of absolute hell, homeless and living out of my car.

On Christmas day, I got mad! I started yelling at myself for what I had allowed to happen. From that day forward, I made a commitment to succeed and to never wind up broke again. On the twenty-eighth day after starting a new venture from the trunk of my car and a pay phone booth, I made $2,000 in 10 hours, then another $6,500 in 30 hours. In my first full-time month, I broke all the company sales records for that international multi-billion-dollar company. I was number one in sales in the world every month after that and made $250,000 my first year with the company. I went on to make my first million the following year by the age of twenty-three.

Now there are some key points to this story that I want to reveal to you that will help your home business become more successful right now:

• Very often, people's objections are only excuses to hide their fears or insecurities. I said "NO" because I didn't think I could do it. Keep this in mind when you get objections from people. Often it's not you or your business they are rejecting, but their own lack of self-confidence.

• Facts tell—stories sell. Stories are critical to your success. I did not become interested until I heard that engineer's story. Stories are the only thing that gets people over the psychological process of "is this simple, does it work, and can I do it?" Facts do not get this job done. Look at your presentations. Are you boring people with the facts? Stories motivate people to buy your product, reorder and join as a representative or distributor in your company. Stories motivate them to go to work and keep trying when they get discouraged and feel like quitting.

• Training—how much money and time does a doctor, lawyer or engineer invest in their education? And how long does it take before they see the rewards or pay off that debt? Be willing to invest in your education for this industry. It will be only a fraction of what most spend on a college education, but the rewards are much greater.

• Never give up, never give in, and never quit! No matter how bad the circumstances, no matter how bad the tragedy, no matter how huge the problems, never ever give up. After being homeless, I became a millionaire in just a couple of years. You never know when your life is going to explode and change forever.

Remember, if a broke homeless cocktail waitress can do it, anyone with a teachable spirit and the desire to succeed can do it, too. So good luck and God bless.

Dani Johnson is an internationally recognized coach, trainer, and author. For more information, go to *www.workathomeprofitzone.com/guerilla*

TACTIC 97. JOINING A MASTER MIND GROUP

Napoleon Hill, author of the bestselling book, *Think and Grow Rich*, originated the idea of the Master Mind group, which he described as "The coordination of knowledge and effort of two or more people, who work toward a definite purpose, in the spirit of harmony. . . . No two minds ever come together without thereby creating a third, invisible intangible force, which may be likened to a third mind."

Join or form a Master Mind group with people who share a mutual interest in success and who will agree to meet on a scheduled day and time—either in person or on the phone—to challenge and support each other in reaching their individual aims.

In Master Mind sessions, members brainstorm strategies, share comments about each other's progress, and become accountable for moving toward individual or group goals. Five to eight people is a good-sized group that will allow everyone a chance to speak. Everyone should share a commitment to be present each meeting and to keep the discussions confidential.

"Sometimes the situation is only a problem because it is looked at in a certain way. Looked at in another way, the right course of action may be so obvious that the problem no longer exists."
~ Edward de Bono ~

Group members will act as sounding boards for new ideas and inspiration for growth. They can give honest and realistic feedback which you might not get from people you already know well. A Master Mind group can quickly become a vital support network that can lift you up when you're feeling down. You can also gain leadership skills out of participation in a Master Mind group by learning self-mastery and coaching others.

The Direct Selling Women's Alliance (www.mydswa.org) offers leader members no-cost entry to a Master Mind group of top direct selling professionals who choose to focus on growing their direct selling businesses. Members with fifty or more people in their organizations can participate on a monthly Master Mind call, which focuses on a specific business-related discussion topic. The Master Mind group is a safe place for members to find solutions to common business challenges as well as share solutions they successfully implemented through their business, thereby improving results and feeling empowered.

A search for "Master Mind groups" or "MasterMind groups" will turn up many pages on the Web that discuss this topic and how to set up a group of your own.

Tactic 98. Continuing Education

A *Harvard Review* article reported that only 10 percent of the population can be called "natural learners"— people who look forward to learning. The other 90 percent view learning as a chore that must be done in order to reach a goal. Since 90 percent of your team may feel resistance toward training, you have to make it fun or no one will choose to do it.

Successful network marketers are voracious learners. You can easily recognize them because they:

• Read every book written on network marketing, knowing that even one single insight can make a profound impact in their compensation.

• Actively schedule personal growth trainings to improve themselves and their skills.

"Learning is an active process. We learn by doing. Only knowledge that is used sticks in your mind."
~ Dale Carnegie ~

• Attend every company convention because of the immense leverage of getting prospects to experience the enthusiasm of thousands of people doing their business.

• Participate on conference calls because it gets everyone on the same page about what's going on with training, products, and compensation bonuses.

• Subscribe to network marketing magazines and newsletters.

• Read consumer magazines devoted to the same audience they seek to reach, and learn about the latest trends, research studies, and competitive products and services.

Internet webinars for educational training make learning convenient. Virtual interactive classrooms like those offered by Networking University (see www.networkingtimes.com) allow teachers to present slides and engage in live chat with students who can ask questions in real time. Class sessions are recorded and can be replayed anytime later. In addition to virtual classes, visitors to Networking University can access more than 200 articles on personal and professional development. Virtual learning by way of webinars can be accessed from all over the world making online education a tool for training team members who live in other countries.

Successful network marketers study marketing tactics of other industries. High earners study and employ marketing methods used by retailers, publishers, Internet marketers, and more industries to learn tactics other distributors aren't using to help their marketing messages stand out.

Just as repeating marketing messages to prospects earns a higher rate of response, repeating training messages stimulates learners to incorporate more of their skills. Training helps you:

- Close more sales
- Build stronger relationships
- Increase your sales volume faster
- Retain customers and distributors
- Feel at ease about your business by improving and adding to your skills
- Set clear goals so you will know exactly where your business is going
- Enable you to help your distributors succeed by passing the training on to them.

Continue your education in network marketing by subscribing to the free *Guerrilla Multilevel Marketing Newsletter* (at www.gmmlm.com) for ongoing support to readers of this book.

Tactic 99. Capitalizing on Your Compensation Plan

You may not yet be thinking of your business as a product, but that is exactly what it is, especially when you are talking to prospective distributors. For them to commit, they must *buy* the opportunity.

Get to know your compensation plan and use it as a marketing tactic. Stay up to date about the latest contests and opportunities so you can pass on news to your team. Remember to get immediate results for new distributors by teaching them how to use the bonus plan to earn the most amount of money in the fastest ways.

When describing your comp plan, keep presentations simple and brief. Don't try to impress someone with all the levels and percentages; you'll have them rolling their eyes in bewilderment. Just highlight the main points which show how to earn money quickly.

The typical comp plan allows distributors to generate income from:

- Retail sales — you earn the profit between the wholesale cost and retail price
- Commission overrides — you get paid commissions on the sales volumes of your organization
- Fast track bonuses — you collect added bonuses for sponsoring new people with special enrollment packs
- Contests — you win vacation or cash prizes based on increase in sales volume over specified period
- Leadership pool — distributors reaching top ranks in the pay plan split additional commissions based on total company sales.

Residual income is not an experience most of the population has ever known. Getting a job and earning a salary is. Trying to convince someone of the benefits of residual income without their having the reality of the experience is like describing an apple to a person who has never tasted one. They have nothing to compare it to.

On the other hand, almost everyone gets excited when they get money in their hands. When looking for ways to motivate new distributors, use your fast track or fast starter bonus to get them a check as quickly as you can. Immediate results will keep them in long enough to eventually come to taste the sweetness of residual income.

TACTIC 100. TRACKING AND MEASURING YOUR RESULTS

Tracking what goes on in your business will increase your comp check, shorten the time it takes to reach your goals, and save you money. Equally important, measuring your marketing results increases your sense of ownership. Tracking puts you in control of your business. Guerrilla marketers track important data in order to:

• Increase marketing tactics that are most profitable.

• Improve marketing tactics that need work.

• Stop marketing tactics that aren't paying off.

• Remove doubt about what's happening with their business.

• Organize business costs for calculating tax deductible expenses at income tax time.

What to Track

• Track your ad results from testing different ad copy and different size ads. Key code the ads or use different websites to record response rates.

• Track the days and times you call leads that you've bought. Are more people signing up if you

Guerrilla Affirmation

I have an **accountability** system in place for myself with my upline for attaining my goals and also for helping my active team members achieve their goals.

call on Wednesday afternoons than on Friday mornings?

• Track your leads to learn if those you bought from one source result in higher sign-ups than another source.

• Track how many follow-ups you make and compare the sign-up numbers. Does it take you an average of eight contacts to get a new distributor?

• Track how many customers you get from trade shows, and use that information to make decisions when planning future events. Compare types of events against each other in order to predict where you'll get the best results.

• Track the money you invest in marketing and compare it to your compensation check. Learn how much it costs you on average to acquire a new customer or a new distributor.

• Track what products customers buy so you can follow up with them with helpful hints or reminders.

Does your MLM provide details of your customer's orders through geneology reports? If they do, you can learn which products a customer has bought regularly in the past, so that if they haven't ordered in a while, you can follow up with a helpful reminder on how they can stop missing their favorite product.

TACTIC 101. PERSISTING WITH YOUR PROMOTIONS

This book promised 100 tactics, but we couldn't leave out one of the most important. Regardless of how many marketing tactics you choose to implement in your business, persisting with your marketing is vital. Persistence means staying with your marketing plan even when nothing apparent is happening. Sometimes it takes months for the accumulated results of your daily marketing activities to manifest.

Commitment
by Sherry Roden

For eleven exciting years, I poured myself into a professional life as associate director of Career Services at Oklahoma State University. I was instrumental in leading the department to grow from five to thirty employees and a budget to grow from $150,000 to $2 million.

The day our son, Zach, was born turned my values and level of professional satisfaction upside down. Since my husband and I had been married for ten years prior to having children, we were quite comfortable living on two salaries and the two-income debt that had accumulated. That comfort quickly turned to a knot in my stomach every time I had to take Zach to daycare. The luster of my career had faded, but it was paramount that I continue to work.

Since I am an efficient administrator who is known for finding systems that work, I knew a solution was sure to be around the corner. It didn't take long to realize that start-up costs for a franchise were enormous. I kept listening and researching for other alternatives—until the day I went to a ladies' Bible study and met a friend who introduced me to the network marketing industry and Arbonne International. After a brief period of experiencing outstanding results, it was a logical conclusion that a home business with Arbonne was indeed my path to work from home while being able to take care of my son, Zach.

While maintaining the full-time career position, I built my business through part-time efforts while also learning invaluable keys to success. My Arbonne activity was indeed a business, and I knew I could not treat it as a hobby. I created a long-term vision, kept a sponge-like teachable attitude, and made consistent efforts in every area. Without these three ingredients, I could not have attained success.

Network marketing is not a fast track to wealth. It takes time, discipline, strategic activity, and persistent effort to achieve desired results. It is practically impossible to grow a business without intentional daily activity. The people who do not achieve their dreams in network marketing are the ones who quit because they do not choose to embrace the necessary commitment.

Since most people who get involved in this industry have no previous experience, there is a learning curve. I decided early on that if I waited until I knew everything, nothing would get off the ground.

I tell myself every day that this is a practice run. I will keep practicing until I see the results I desire, and will ride the natural highs and lows, which arrive in all forms of noble efforts. The people who stay committed during the highs and lows are rewarded for their patience and consistent effort.

Nothing has personally challenged me and served to develop my effective life skills more than the opportunity of network marketing. The icing on the cake has been the amazing income potential. It grows day by day, and I get to drive a white Mercedes-Benz, compliments of Arbonne.

Sherry Roden is Regional Vice President and Independent Consultant with Arbonne International. Learn more at <u>www.sherryroden.myarbonne.com</u>.

Checklist for this Chapter's Tactics

Place a check in the appropriate column for determining how or if you will use a tactic. Then return to your 7-sentence marketing plan - see Chapter 3 - and fill in the appropriate tactics in Step 4 of your plan.

Tactics In This Chapter	Using Well	Using, But Needs Work	Not Using	Not Right At This Time
94. Providing Good Service				
95. Becoming Accountable				
96. Associating with Successful People				
97. Joining a Mastermind Group				
98. Continuing Education				
99. Capitalizing on Your Comp Plan				
100. Tracking and Measuring Results				
101. Persisting				

CHAPTER 20

WHAT TO DO NEXT

"It's the little things you do that can make a big difference. What are you attempting to accomplish? What little thing can you do today that will make you more effective? You are probably only one step away from greatness."
~ Bob Proctor ~

Many network marketers linger too long in the planning mode. They take the trainings, get on conference calls, but somehow never move into taking action. If you have team members who seem stuck, go through action steps with them for the first week or ten days. Be there like a patient parent, just long enough for them to experience what it's like to implement new activities, step-by-step.

Taking baby steps is the key. It's where real momentum happens. When too many tasks are planned, a person is unlikely to take any action. Small tasks are easier. And having someone there with you enlivens the learning and makes it fun.

The Plan for Acting on Your Plan

If you've read this book all the way through, you are aware of a multitude of marketing avenues at your disposal. What should you do first? And then next, and so on?

1. Get familiar with your products or services. If they've changed your life, write those experiences

down. Be ready to tell your story at a moment's notice. Know the highlights of your bonus plan, statistics about your market, and the benefits your product or service offers.

2. Learn how to use the Internet and other technologies to cut your costs, automate your communications, and speed your ability to interact with people daily.

3. Go back to your 7-sentence marketing plan and refine your list of benefits. Then, highlight the benefits that competing products or services don't talk about. These are the key benefits to include in your marketing material.

4. From your 7-sentence plan, prioritize the tactics you will use. Take your time. Don't try to set all your tactics into motion at once; do what you can do within your situation.

5. Create your guerrilla marketing calendar where you list your activities, their costs, and the dates you will take action.

6. When considering tactics, look at ways to best leverage your time. How can you reach the greatest number of people in the shortest period? How many distributors can you realistically support?

7. Learn how much activity feels comfortable and invest only the amount of money you can afford.

8. Don't give up if you fail to see immediate returns. Some tactics (such as home parties) produce instant income, while other forms of marketing (such as display ads) take time. It is consistent and persistent marketing that pays off.

9. Use your guerrilla marketing calendar to keep track of your results, which will be visible by how much your comp check goes up. Measure your results against what you invested.

10. Every three months, evaluate the results you are getting. Do more of those tactics which take you toward your goal. Tweak approaches that are giving you mediocre results. Eliminate activities that don't work.

"A successful life is one that is lived through understanding and pursuing one's own path, not chasing after the dreams of others."
~ Chin-Ning Chu ~

It's vital for you to set your own criteria for how you will grow. Because we sometimes get in the habit of relying on our upline or company, it is easy to slip into nonconsciously taking on their goals, instead of getting clear about our own.

We're more likely to act when we're passionate about aims we truly value. And since taking action is the most important thing you can do in your business, get clear about what's most important to you, so that you will do whatever it takes and be happy to do it because it means something to you.

Keith McEachern's story may give you a new perspective moving toward your goals. There's really no excuse when your aim is clear and important.

No Excuses
by Keith McEachern

Even in my early twenties, I had a flare for guerrilla marketing. I used to light myself on fire (literally) on street corners to sell fire extinguishers. From there, I got into fire alarms and then into security systems. From that point on, my business life was devoted to developing residual income. You see, when you sell a burglar system one time, people pay you forever more for the monitoring of the alarm system.

There came a time, however, when the security business was not much fun, what with regulatory interference and liabilities. I sold the company and, as a young single guy with a lot of dollars in his pocket—and not a lot of sense— I traveled the world, partied, and squandered the money.

Landing in Jamaica, I got involved with a local island beauty. In the course of time, she revealed that she tried to enrich her poor life by pushing small amounts of marijuana into the U.S. I really had no heart for making illicit money, nor did I have a taste for the drug. However, I was moved to help her in small ways. Three years down the road, I found myself enmeshed in a lifestyle which left me feeling guilt, fear, and self-loathing. I was a lost soul. Then I did what scared boys do—I ran away. Returned home and tried to act like nothing had happened. I prayed for a good woman and God sent me my wife, Pam.

One day seven years later, I was sitting in the house we were building, nestled in the quiet woods of Connecticut. Suddenly, armed lawmen in several cars pulled up. They advised me I was being arrested for conspiracy back in 1983 to smuggle and distribute marijuana for sale. My sins had finally caught up with me.

While out on bail, I got a visit from two MLM friends, Ray Faltinsky and Kevin Fournier, who had no idea of my situation. They shared their vision for FreeLife, a new company they desired to build, and, more importantly, the kind of ideals they would stand for. We agreed that I would be their founding distributor. But as my trial date neared, I knew I had to come clean. I related my story to Ray and Kevin, told them it was likely I would be imprisoned. But my greatest fear was the heartbreak that would come by leaving my wife and my precious son behind. I assumed I'd get walking papers. Instead, Kevin and Ray came through with courage, love, and acceptance. They agreed it might be a rough road, but they had made their choice and they would stand by me.

Ray said that he would come to the sentencing to make a case before the judge. He spoke on my behalf, as did others, including my wife, Pam. The judge listened and then announced I would serve 30 months in Federal Prison. He gave me 24 days to put my affairs in order.

Here's what I did. "Look," I said to Pam, "we can cry all month over ourselves, but I have 24 days to build a business. I'm going to spend every hour of every day on the phone until I fall over in my chair."

I had a list of names of my network and of business cards collected from laundromat bulletin boards and everywhere else I could find people who might listen to a business opportunity. I asked people for the names of others, offering to speak to them and learn if they were open-minded about extra income. In those 24 days, I talked to 1,500 people and recruited 44 distributors.

Leaving my group in Kevin and Ray's hands, I reported to prison to begin serving my sentence. Though I went behind bars, income to my family started coming in. Their first month's check was $1,000; the second month's $4,000; the third month's $7,000; and the fourth month's $10,217.

On the inside, prison was everything it's advertised to be. But one day I saw this gray-haired pot-bellied Italian guy with a big cigar in hand sipping a cup of espresso. I commented to him that it looked like his time here wasn't so difficult. He assured me it wasn't and asked me where I was living. I told him. "Oh you're in the Zoo!" he said.

He took me around some stairs and down into a basement—into an area I didn't even know existed. It was like a country club; a bunch of white-haired Italian guys, all whispering to each other. He explained that the warden's idea of a good prison was clean, polished floors. My old friend related how he was just too old and unable to polish his floor and get points from the warden. He needed help. The next day, I was somehow transferred to the country club.

I shined this guy's floor and the floors for all the old Italian guys. When the warden realized I was the guy responsible for the polished paradise, I suggested that I could even make the telephone room, which was a mess and eyesore, a polished beauty. I told him that if he could rope it off for four hours every day, his job as a good warden could be complete.

That prisoner's telephone room became my telephone room for four hours a day. I worked as fast as I could on my hands and knees to be able to make calls when my job was done. I made calls to my network to introduce them to the company and get them to attend meetings around the country.

Business calls in prison were not allowed. At the risk of being thrown in the hole and losing even daylight, I made the calls anyway. My family's future depended on it.

In one instance, I'd arranged for five prospects to attend a meeting in Baltimore. I told a woman, recruited by me before I went into prison, to pick up my five prospects and take them to the meeting; she could enroll them wherever she pleased. She whined about how difficult it would be for her with her busy schedule to drive an hour to get to the meeting. The next day I called and she complained that only four of my five showed up and she only recruited three of the four. I asked how many people she herself had brought to the meeting. None! Lots of reasons why not.

"Life must be tough out there, where you have nothing but freedom," I thought to myself. "I'm in here under scrutiny, having all freedoms removed. Are there really excuses that serve anyone? If only I had my freedom, how much more I could choose to do."

When I got out and fully engaged again in FreeLife, I realized that I had to make friends fast. The best way I knew how to do it was by helping others. Rather than sponsor for myself, I sponsored for others. But you know what happens in this business when you help others achieve their dreams? You achieve your own.

Today, my organization stretches around the globe, earning my family over $250,000 a month and more freedom than most people ever dream of.

What's your excuse? Do YOU have the freedom to build your business, or have you put yourself in a mental prison? If you've got any kind of black hole in your life, put it behind you now and start over. Embrace the price and give thanks for the opportunity to do so.

Keith McEachern is a network marketing trainer and the founding master distributor with FreeLife (www.freelife.com.)

"If I had to select one quality, one personal characteristic that I regard as being most highly correlated with success, whatever the field, I would pick the trait of persistence. Determination. The will to endure to the end, to get knocked down seventy times and get up off the floor saying, "Here comes number seventy-one!""
~ Richard DeVos, co-founder Amway ~

You've got a dream, you've got a plan, you've got strategies. Now it's time to weave the elements of the big picture together by taking action.

For a quick start, pick just three tactics from this book and then rank them first, second, and third. Write down the action steps you will take for these tactics in your marketing calendar. Set the date for taking action, starting today.

Now go do it. Tomorrow, do three more marketing actions, and so on every day.

If you do just three marketing actions a day for thirty days, you'll develop the guerrilla marketing mindset and be on your way to getting real and measurable results—meaning fatter checks your family is waiting to spend for you.

Go guerrilla go!

RESOURCES

21-Day Guerrilla Action Plan

With the purchase of this book, you are entitled to receive the *21-Day Guerrilla Action Plan* free. Each day for three weeks, you'll receive an action step by e-mail to help you make the most of the *Guerrilla Multilevel Marketing* system. To claim your Action Plan, see www.gmmlm.com/21days/.

www.GMMLM.com

The *Guerrilla Multilevel Marketing* website helps keep you up to date with new trends in promoting your network marketing / direct selling business. We bring you the latest tools for finding qualified leads and bringing them into your warm list.

Guerrilla Multilevel Marketing Newsletter

Subscribe for free to the *Guerrilla Multilevel Marketing Newsletter*. Every month, you can access news and tactics for growing your compensation. Get practical solutions for finding and converting prospects. Subscribe for free and without risk. We don't share your e-mail with other parties and you can unsubscribe at any time. Subscribe at www.gmmlm.com.

Guerrilla Marketing Coach Certification™

Instantly brand yourself with the best-selling marketing series in history with the *Guerrilla Marketing Coach Certification™*. Increase your revenue by adding guerrilla marketing and coaching to your skill set. Gain access into the guerrilla marketing coaches alumni forum. Join an intensive 12-week program designed to hold you accountable to attracting new customers and increasing your active compensation. See www.gmmlm.com/coach/.

What To Do When Your People Stop Recruiting

Have you run out of people to talk to? Tired of leads that don't work? Get interested, HOT leads, along with training to call them back. We provide the tools and training on more than 23 different guerrilla ways to generate an ongoing supply of new, warm market leads that you ordinarily would not come in contact with. See www.gmmlm.com/leads/.

Magazines

Home Business Connection: www.hbcmag.com
MLM Magazine (Australia): www.mlmaustralia.com.au
Network Marketing Business Journal: www.nmbj.com
Network Marketing Times: www.networkingtimes.com
Opportunity World: www.oppworld.com
The Network Marketing Magazine:
 www.thenetworkmarketingmagazine.com

Newsletters

Find Your Why: www.findyourwhy.com
I Love MLM Letter: www.ilovemlm.com
MLM Insider: www.mlminsider.com
MLM Woman Newsletter: www.mlmwoman.com

Tools

Direct Marketing Association List of Resources:
 www.thedirectmarketingsearch.com
INTI Publishing: www.intipublishing.com
Sound Concepts: www.soundconcepts.com
VideoPlus: www.videoplus.com
VMDirect: www.yourbusinessvideos.com
Wellness Success Media: www.wellnesssuccessmedia.com

Lead Providers

A Guerrilla Leads System: www.gmmlm.com/leads/
Cutting Edge Media: www.cuttingedgemedia.com
Elite MLM Leads: www.elitemlmleads.com

Exclusive MLM Leads: www.exclusivemlmleads.com
Fast MLM Leads: www.fastmlmleads.com
Jungle Leads: www.jungleleads.com
Instant Leads: www.instantleads.com
LeadsLab MLM leads: www.leadslab.com
Leaders Club MLM leads: www.leadersclub.com
Leads2yoursuccess: www.leads2yoursuccess.com
Live Leads: www.liveleadstore.com
MLM leads.com: www.mlmleads.com
Networkleads: www.networkleads.com
NPros: www.npros.com
Optimized Leads: www.optimizedleads.com
Peak Impact: www.peakimpact.com
Power Lead Source: www.powerleadsource.com
Traffic Oasis: www.trafficoasis.com
Sherpa Leads: www.sherpaleads.com

Trainers

Art Jonak: www.mlmplayers.com
Bob Proctor: www.bobproctor.com
Bonnie Ross-Parker: www.thejoyofconnecting.com
Dale Calvert: www.mlmhelp.com
Dani Johnson: www.danijohnson.com
Doug Firebaugh: www.passionfire.com
Dr. Joe Rubino: www.centerforpersonalreinvention.com
Hilton and Lisa Johnson: www.mlmu.com
Janet Larson: www.janetpossible.com
Janine Avila: www.janineavila.com
Jeffery Combs: www.goldenmastermind.com
Jerry Clark: www.clubrhino.com
John Milton Fogg: www.greatestnetworker.com
Kim Klaver: www.whowho911.com
Kosta Gara: www.kostagara.com
Lorna Rasmussen: www.absolutebestway.com
Marcella Vonn Harting: www.marcellavonnharting.com
Margie Aliprandi: www.crowndiamond.net
Michael Clouse: www.nexera.com
Mike Limere: www.mlmdevelopment.com
Networking University: www.networkingtimes.com/university

Paula Pritchard and Kathy Robbins: mlmmadesimple.com
Randy Gage: www.networkmarketingtimes.com
Richard Brooke: www.richardbrooke.com
Rita Davenport: www.ritadavenport.com
Robert Butwin: www.streetsmartlive.com
Tim Sales: www.brilliantexchange.com
Todd Falcone: www.toddfalcone.com
Tom "Big Al" Schreiter: www.fortunenow.com

Associations

Direct Selling Women's Alliance: www.dswa.org
111 Hekili St., Suite A139, Kailua, HI 96734
Phone: (888) 417-0743
The DSWA's mission is to be a welcoming community to direct selling professionals who share a common vision of personal and financial success through their home-based business. For cutting edge training, trusted resources, and high level networking and support, learn more about this world-wide association dedicated to the success and empowerment of their members.

Direct Selling Association: www.dsa.org
1667 K Street, NW Suite 100
Washington DC, DC 20006-1660
Phone: (202) 452-8866
Direct Selling Association is a national association of over 150 direct sales companies. Their mission is to protect, serve and promote the effectiveness of member companies and the independent business people they represent.

Multilevel Marketing International Assn: www.mlmia.com
11956 Bernardo Plaza Suite 313
San Diego, CA 92128
Phone: (760) 630-6287
MLMIA is a trade association, started in 1985 by industry professionals for Network Marketing Companies, the Distributors who sell a Company's goods and services to the end consumer and suppliers to the industry.

The Guerrilla Marketiang Association
www.guerrillamarketingassociation.com
714 Sawyer St. SE
Olympia, WA 98501
Phone: 1-800-748-6444
The Guerrilla Marketing Association is an interactive small business marketing support system that puts you in direct contact with Jay Conrad Levinson, The Father of Guerrilla Marketing and his cadre of trained Guerrilla Marketing Coaches. Membership includes monthly online reports filled with marketing tips and video interviews, a weekly newsletter, weekly live teleclasses, live chats, and a forum board to post and get answers to your business questions.

ABOUT THE AUTHORS

Jay Conrad Levinson is the author of the best-selling marketing series in history, *Guerrilla Marketing*, plus 24 other business books. His guerrilla concepts have influenced marketing so much that today his books appear in 41 languages and are required reading in many MBA programs worldwide.

Jay taught guerrilla marketing for ten years at the University of California in Berkeley. And he was a practitioner of it in the United States as Senior Vice-President at J. Walter Thompson and in Europe as Creative Director at Leo Burnett Advertising.

Jay has served on the Microsoft Small Business Council and the 3Com Small Business Advisory Board. His Guerrilla Marketing is series of books, a videotape, an award-winning CD-ROM, a newsletter, a consulting organization, an Internet website and a way for you to spend less, get more and achieve substantial profits.

James Dillehay reached Diamond level in his network marketing program. He is author of eight books, a former magazine publisher and editor, marketing coach, and seminar leader. He is a nationally recognized expert on helping people with big dreams and small budgets generate income streams successfully.

James' books and articles have been recommended by *The Chicago Tribune, Family Circle, The Whole Earth Catalog, Better Homes & Gardens, Working Mothers, The National Examiner, Country Almanac* and many more. He has been listed in *Who's Who of American Entrepreneurs*.

As a Certified Guerrilla Marketing Coach, he has helped individuals and organizations learn how to leverage their existing assets into bigger profits using guerrilla strategies.

Marcella Vonn Harting is an internationally recognized author, speaker, facilitator, and entrepreneur. Over the last 15 years, Marcella Vonn built two highly successful network marketing distributorships with more than 200,000 representatives worldwide.

A Crown Diamond, Marcella has achieved the highest rank in her network marketing compensation plan and is one of the top earners in her company, Marcella teaches how to achieve network marketing success in the U.S., Canada, Australia, Japan, and throughout Europe.

In network marketing, she demonstrates how creating a residual abundant income centered in health and wealth can empower balance and purpose in one's life.

Marcella Vonn is an inspirational mentor in manifesting and teaching how to achieve one's highest goals with grace, ease and fun. She resides in Paradise Valley, Arizona with her husband, daughter and son.

INDEX

C

D

E

F

G

H

I

J

K

L

M

N

O

P

R

Notes

Notes

Notes